*After*
TRANSFORMATION

¤ \ ¤ / ¤

*After*
TRANSFORMATION

¤ \ ¤ / ¤

A Lyrical History of
Christian Late Antiquity

MAIA KOTROSITS

Duke University Press   *Durham and London*   2025

© 2025 DUKE UNIVERSITY PRESS. All rights reserved.
Project Editor: Bird Williams
Designed by Courtney Leigh Richardson
Typeset in Minion Pro and Cronos by Copperline Book Services

Library of Congress Cataloging-in-Publication Data
Names: Kotrosits, Maia, author.
Title: After transformation : a lyrical history of Christian late antiquity / Maia Kotrosits.
Description: Durham : Duke University Press, 2025. | Includes bibliographical references and index.
Identifiers: LCCN 2025013985 (print)
LCCN 2025013986 (ebook)
ISBN 9781478032762 (paperback)
ISBN 9781478029328 (hardcover)
ISBN 9781478061540 (ebook)
Subjects: LCSH: Church history—Primitive and early church, ca. 30–600. | Christianity and culture—History—Early church, ca. 30–600. | Imperialism—Religious aspects—History. | Emotions—Religious aspects. | COVID-19 Pandemic, 2020–2023—Religious aspects.
Classification: LCC BR170 .K687 2025 (print)
LCC BR170 (ebook)
LC record available at https://lccn.loc.gov/2025013985
LC ebook record available at https://lccn.loc.gov/2025013986

Cover art: *Textile Fragment with a Leaf*, fourth century, Egypt. Wool, linen, 12 1/16 inch × 9 1/16 inch. Metropolitan Museum of Art, New York. Purchased by subscription, 1889. metmuseum.org.

We Did Not Go to the Ruins at Ostia

We went instead to the beach with the black sand. It was the hottest day of summer and the sand was so scorching we had to leave our shoes at the edge of the water, everyone on the beach did, hundreds of flip flops nearly swept out by the waves. We laughed when we finally got in, we had made it past the gauntlet of umbrellas and chairs, weaving and bounding with the least steps we could manage. The sea was so salty it burned our eyes, we squinted at each other, still laughing, gasping for breath. We were swimming with grouper that could swallow my leg, and later we got pizza by the pound, and ate it while we stood on the pavement. We rode the train back to the city with hair and clothes wet, watching the car fill up and the sun get orange and low. We were quiet, glutted, only at the beginning. Two historians, in Rome for work, and we didn't see the ancient theater, the statues of the entwined wrestlers, the overgrown gardens. We didn't see the bath of Mithras or the church that was built on top. We did not want the past, its plight and its rot. We held another time, larger, more ludicrous, in our arms.

# Contents

Acknowledgments ix
Introduction 1
Prologue 23

¤ \ ¤ / ¤

PART I: **Fathers** 27
Interlude: On the Origin of the World 49

¤ \ ¤ / ¤

PART II: **Notes from the Interior** 51
Interlude: The Phoenix 67

¤ \ ¤ / ¤

PART III: **Saints' Lives** 69
Interlude: On First Principles 93

¤ \ ¤ / ¤

PART IV: **The Passing World**     95

¤ \ ¤ / ¤

Epilogue     119
Appendix     121
Notes     129
Bibliography     143

Acknowledgments

I wrote this book in a lot of solitude and a lot of community. I felt the gravity and immensity of both. I am grateful to the many academic colleagues and acquaintances whose ideas, friendship, generosity, and trust held me over the years I wrote this book. I took none of them for granted. Some of those people, but certainly not all, are named below.

I am also grateful to have had institutional support from the University of Waterloo Department of Classical Studies (especially Altay Coskun and David Porreca), the University of Toronto Department for the Study of Religion (especially Pamela Klassen and John Marshall), and the Harvard Center for the Study of World Religions (especially Charles Stang), while this book was in process. My conversations with my colleagues at HDS and the CSWR were especially lively and fortifying. I workshopped material for this book at the "Experiencing Insecurity: Pain, Trauma, and Suffering in the Roman Empire" conference at Boston University, and at the University of Minnesota Center for Premodern Studies. Those attentive audiences helped me understand this book all the better. Thanks, in particular, to the press's reviewers for the profound satisfaction of the seriousness of their engagement with an unusual manuscript.

Deepest gratitude to Miriam Angress, for believing there was something here. Haifa Staiti, for unlocking the little cage. Tim Beal, for first showing me academics could be *writers*. Sarit Kattan Gribetz and David Maldonado Rivera, for tinkering with time. Burke Gerstsenschlager, for sending me Fiona Benson poems. Mike Chin, Cavan Concannon, Jenny Knust, Kyle Wagner, Sarah Porter, Cláudio Carvalhaes, and Sarah Curtin, for hearing the pings in this idea. Martie Roberts, Spencer Dew, and Cristina Caldari for being companionable misfits with me. Heidi Wendt, Jen McGuire, and Colleen Shantz, for sewing up my ripped seams. Eric Smith, for assuring me of how conventional I am. Rhiannon Graybill, for your generous imagination, and for the resounding yes. Erin Runions, Benny Liew, Katie Lofton, John Modern, Zsuzsa Varhelyi, Dan-el Padilla Peralta, and most especially Mahri Leonard-Fleckman, for always seeing the best in my work. Andrew Jacobs, for calling up the most haunted late antiquity. Ryan Schellenberg, for illuminating this manuscript and entering its world so wholly. Greg Given, for your hunger for all the little backstories. Alexis Waller, for dreaming up the "creativity book" years ago. Joseph Kotrosits and Cathy Cappel, for your faith in time and me. Jean Kotrosits, for singing "Que Sera Sera." Lynn Shelly, for your secret poems in the downstairs filing cabinet, and for teaching me, very early, to write from my experience. Rocco Russo, for your matchless spirit, and for writing your own poems at my side. Celene Lillie, for your constancy and humor and wisdom through it all. Marion Ramirez, for laughing through disaster together, for teaching me the dance between moon and earth, for creating with me a corner of the world we could live in. Carly Daniel-Hughes and Michal Beth Dinkler, for knowing how to be in the abyss bravely. For keeping me in your warmth. For being right there for every single painstaking line, and what it took to make it. Phil Harland, for always knowing what matters most. And for making so much possible, including this.

## Introduction

THINGS ARE BREAKING

> Who will speak these days,
> if not I,
> if not you?
> —MURIEL RUKEYSER,
> "The Speed of Darkness"

This book is a lyrical history of Christian late antiquity. It began when I reread Peter Brown's *The Making of Late Antiquity* for the first time in a decade, alongside a lot of poetry, during the first several months of the pandemic. Passing through different forms of consciousness about the newly visible extremity of the world I occupied, buried in my own extremity of sickness and isolation,[1] trapped in the interminable and achingly terminal era that I had no idea was coming, I found myself desperate for some form of expression that met the moment. Poetry makes immediate sense for experiences so monumental and disorienting. Brown's book, which attempts to capture the large-scale changes of the second through fourth centuries, an era in which Christian language, practices, and conceptualities became central to Roman elite culture and imperial rule, consequently ushering in its own idiosyncratic colonialism, seems perhaps a less likely go-to. But it was the way that Brown began that carried me through the entirety of the book: "I wish that I had been one of the Seven Sleepers of Ephesus," he writes, in a conceit that would, from then on, provide the subtext for nearly all proceeding understandings of this period.[2] These seven Christian brothers fell asleep in a cave during the middle of the third century, so one version of the story goes, hiding from violence against Christians under Decius. They stretched and awoke a century or so later only to find themselves in a world they could hardly recognize: a Christian one. "Imagine their surprise," Brown muses, as they stepped into a terrain so palpably changed. He casts his book as "an attempt to enter into their surprise" at the remarkable shifts of (especially) the third century, to look with fresh eyes at what has, since Brown's book, become the most definitive way of understanding late antiquity as such: its transformations.

Amazed that I hadn't remembered how charming Brown's prose is, or what a complete world he unfolds for his reader, I immediately identified with Brown, and with the seven sleepers, but with a wildly different valence: head fogged, body crushed with exhaustion and ripped with anxiety, I wanted nothing more than to go to bed and stay there indefinitely. Then to wake up, someday, in a new world.

Fresh off my last book, which felt at the time like a massive expenditure I could never repeat, and (frankly) mad at the conventions of academic prose for being so spiritless and stolid when life was reminding us repeatedly, gravely, of the stakes of how we conduct ourselves, I could not bring myself to write much in any form other than poems. Or, at first, pieces of poems—little poetic phrases or images that didn't belong to any larger thought I could yet articulate. I returned once again to texts and figures of late antiquity, but this time with a sense that there was some profound consonance between the present and the past: the disorientation and lostness, the attempts to come to grips with grief, mass death, and magnified physical vulnerability, the struggle to understand time and change. Both times defined by Christian imperialism.[3] The writing that resulted was the only writing that could hold these consonances and raw experiences reasonably well.

This book, then, critically redescribes central phenomena and figures of Christian late antiquity—saints and ascetics, Origen and Augustine, Christian pilgrimage, for example—but does so by taking cues from this elongated condition of blurriness and heightened attunement, by staying with it even as the specificity of the urgencies revised themselves.[4] It does this retelling via a collection of lyrical forms ranging from micro-essay to lyrical vignette to poem to fragment. It represents a set of conjunctions and interrelations, often nonliteral or oblique ones, between distant past and extended present so as to reexperience both.

One of the book's primary aims is to depict historical relationships between Christians and imperialism with new intricacy and dimension, and create a small dossier tracing some of the vast violence and profound effects of Christian colonialism in and across time and place. Historian Jeremy Schott has already shown how late ancient Christian apologetic discourses, which were ethnographic and racializing discourses, were fundamental epistemological frameworks for early European conquest and colonization, ones which continued to underwrite nineteenth- and twentieth-century comparative and world religions projects.[5] While this book seeks more furtive, and more immanent, connections than these, it assumes the force of these pasts.

Of course this book does intervene, sometimes explicitly, sometimes implicitly, in scholarly narratives of Christian late antiquity—not least the predominant notion of this period as a period of "transformation." (The "after" in the title *After Transformation* registers this critique.) However this book also takes Christian late antiquity and its resonance in and with the present as an occasion to consider more: the ambiguities of change, desires for sovereign agency and for magnificent self-transformation, and the collapse of those desires. It articulates through historical particulars a phenomenology of the tensions of time, and it asks after the various forms that grief takes in the face of mass death and mundane structural violence. Perhaps most, it is about the ironies of the ways history is written in the face of the ways history is lived.

I write equally for those very familiar with the figures and texts of Christian late antiquity, those with some curiosity about that history who might appreciate an unconventional primer or reading companion, and those who simply long for unorthodox models of writing history. I hint to readers across the humanities that Christian late antiquity can be theoretically interesting and relevant far beyond Foucault's narrow reading and imagination for it,[6] and make some beginning suggestions about how. This book represents my effort to claim resonance, urgency, expressiveness, and even vulnerability for historical work on antiquity. It additionally considers the many small deaths of academic professionalization, and ways to reenvision the potentials of expertise. Beneath it all are questions of time and change: the unfoldings and interruptions of time, the narration and disappointments of change, the relationship of time and change to living and understanding imperialism and colonialism.

Poetry and late antiquity are in some ways long companions. Patricia Cox Miller has highlighted a "poetic imagination" in late ancient literature—a penchant for image, for metaphor, for philosophizing about language among its writers.[7] Maybe this is what begets the dreamy lyricism in not only Brown's work, but Patricia Cox Miller's own writing, as well as the poetic prose of a small handful of other scholars of late antiquity.[8] It is what I have elsewhere described as "lyrical historiography," seen also in the work of Virginia Burrus, Catherine Michael Chin, and Michael Motia.[9] It could very well be that the poetic imagination of late antiquity is what drew these expressive writers to the study. In any case, it is in part the quiet tradition and sly invitations of these writers across time that I take up.[10]

But there is more to this project than: "Can you mix lyricism with late antiquity?" And lyricism is not just about elegant writing. It is about knowledge-production. Academic prose knows some things well, and some things badly.[11] Though you wouldn't believe the latter from academic prose's vast overreach, its attempt to render every corner of the world, era of history, human experience, and act of speculation, into its form. There is nothing that academic prose claims it can't handle. But along with different forms of writing come different kinds of understanding. This project is one experiment in what comes of lyrical knowing.

### Lyricism and Disciplinary Life

In a tantalizing way many individuals have experienced just enough creative living to recognize that for most of their time they are living uncreatively, as if caught up in the creativity of someone else, or of a machine. —D. W. WINNICOTT, *Playing and Reality*

Poetry was an old practice that started when I was a kid, and took a long pause, about fifteen years long, for the part of my adulthood in which I became an academic. Returning to it the last few years highlighted for me how circumscribed the life of lyrical language is in ancient studies, religious studies, and biblical studies (the primary fields from which I speak). "Art" or literariness might be something to study or analyze, and elegant writing might be valued so long as it is guided by refinement of style over affective charge. But lyrical writing can fast become suspicious: "indulgent," "excessive," "opaque." Poetry itself also might serve as a kind of accoutrement: poetry as epigraph, as preface, as evidence of literariness and well-bred education. It becomes a stylized gesture of selection. But this is even while poetry lives a less sterile life on unofficial registers. It is what I've texted friends (or, if you like, the more respectable "colleagues") early in the morning, what we read softly to ourselves when we can't stand any more philological analyses or flat renditions of information. It is what many of us return to at heightened or elemental moments—love, wonder, sickness, death.

So what to make of this contrast? What induces such a self-conscious— wrong word—*controlled* deployment of lyricism on official registers? Here's one thought: lyrical language is the claimed expressiveness these fields want but have mostly given up in their (also highly stylized) emergence as modern fields of study. It is, in other words, what you sell to afford your expertise. Lyricism becomes threat, its pleasures and thickness of meaning shaved down to a canon of acceptable uses, parlayed into the exoticism and mystical air of "other languages," and sometimes even becoming, in this whittled form, its own delicate dispatch.[12]

I tripped into academic life. I entered a biblical studies classroom at the age of twenty-six—an actor, sort of, and a well-intentioned but disillusioned Brooklyn public school teacher. I was still an adolescent, so numbed and melancholy from a long series of acute disasters, personal and collective, that I could barely even register that they were there. I was just simply *curious*, not seeking a career, not even wanting a degree. I felt intuitively obligated to old Christian things, without knowing why, in which ways, or to what ends.

I was also a self-fashioned poet: a creative writing major in college, who had been enabled, fortunately, by a professor who saw writing—and specifically my writing—less as an exercise in perfection of technique than as a venue for an almost perverse attachment to life, even and especially at life's strangest, most inscrutable turns. She'd register me in her graduate poetry workshops, and scribble encouragements that now seem outlandish, like "Send this to Alice Quinn at the *New Yorker*," in the white space next to my Anne Sexton knock-offs, poems caked in my rage and depression. At the same time, she regularly dropped some of the most efficiently terrifying writing advice I've received to date. Once: "Write from what you love, not from what you hate." In this, she taught me the art of grieving.

So it was a sharp turn into the literary world after graduation as I sent my poems out for review, with the attendant waiting and rejections. I got a job with a nonprofit poetry organization in Manhattan, working alongside students in Columbia University's MFA program, and met Alice Quinn who, I learned, did not want my poems for the *New Yorker*. I mispronounced names, earnestly quoted lines back to their writers, and asked, with real confusion, "What do you mean by 'language poets,' aren't all poets language poets?" to George Plimpton himself, longtime editor of the vaunted *Paris Review*, at a cocktail party in his apartment. (Hint: no, they are not.)

I was "unsophisticated." I had not been initiated into the elite forms of knowledge and careful postures that the literary world assumed.[13] Writing, for me, had always been what you might call spiritual. It would be easy to say that I was not "prepared" by my professors to survive the literary world. It's true. They were, to their credit, more discerning than that. And I did not survive the literary world—or rather, I knew something in me *would* not survive there, and so I made a fast exit. Ironically, it was not long after that I found myself plunged into another world with an even steeper price of entry, and an almost endless list of words and names I would flub and forget, usually in public. But what field of study could better accommodate a perverse attachment to life than religion? What is history if not an attempt to fish out or pronounce life's strangest, most inscrutable turns? It was at a conference six months after my defense when I heard for the first time: *What you write is beautiful, but it is not history*. Many versions followed.

While lyricism may be a more obvious interruption of the carefully honed empiricism and self-seriousness of historical fields, the fields of biblical studies and religious studies have their own long contexts for wariness. Biblical studies, for instance, has had a strained and strange relationship to theology: it has consistently wobbled between, on the one hand, its exegetical investments in a slim canon of texts read too often in isolation and, on the other, its desire to cull the legitimacy of proper history via historical critical methods and regular, if arm's length, courting of classics. The becoming of religion as a modern field of study demanded distance between those analyzing and those doing, a distinction between observer and participant.[14] But in all cases lyricism threatens to overtake this carefully assembled creature, the Scholar, with captivation and un-self-consciousness. Lyricism is, in Mark Doty's words, a "slipping ... into the interior landscape of reverie."[15] It might be literary elegance ("musicality"), but it is more definitely getting carried away, the lostness of a child daydreaming.[16] By necessity, then, it is a refusal to wear the proper bearing of detachment. In other words, lyricism looks too much like devotion.[17]

What's more, lyricism can resist, or at least slow down, the commodification of ideas. It obstructs information-making, knowledge in quantified form. It is not strictly productive, at least not in the neoliberal sense. Lyricism is also antiprocedural. It is not a method, and religious studies and biblical studies, in particular, define themselves through method.[18] Indeed, even where poetry and these fields might seem to express compatible interests, these fields distinguish themselves by devising clunky and elaborate systems. Take, for instance, "description," or better yet, *comparison*: where lyricism invites imagination, the open-ended likening of disparate things through metaphor, religious studies invents a machinery, dedicating no small amount of meticulous work and exorbitant worry over its ideal execution.[19]

I point this out not in the name of multi- or interdisciplinarity, since belonging to multiple disciplines often just means multiple forms of deviance—or multiple forms of disenfranchisement. In fact, I begin with this story of my life in the literary world because I want to disentangle lyricism from its formalization and professionalization in the discipline of literary studies. In other words, rather than simply valorizing movements across disciplines (work which I do), I'm more interested in how lyricism is creative play, is therefore the conceptual opposite of "discipline," and how it undermines disciplinarity of all kinds. In other words, I'm interested in how it interrupts our professionalization.

The structured scarcity of contemporary academic life has raised the premium on our professionalization. Many of us have come to imagine professionalization—the constant enactment of a specialized skill set, a certain air of hypercompetence, an enthusiastic alignment with institutional goals and disciplinary creeds—as a route to our security. It might be, sometimes, for some of us. But this woefully overestimates the possibility of guaranteeing our own security. In fact, the very promise of security through tireless and unremitting demonstrations of professionalization is exactly the ruse that prevents intellectual life from doing strange and extraordinary things, from outgrowing its container.

What's more, consider what's at stake: "It is creative apperception more than anything else that makes the individual feel that life is worth living," psychologist D. W. Winnicott writes in *Playing and Reality*. "Contrasted with this is a relationship to external reality which is one of compliance, the world and its details being recognized but only as something to be fitted in with or demanding adaptation." Compliance gives way to a sense of "futility," of deadness, according to Winnicott, but more than that, against creativity's health, "compliance is a sick basis for life."[20]

### "The Hegemony of Reason"

Dry, informational narration. Distant, even transcendent in tone, inflected by specialized vocabulary (*comparanda*, for instance) and careful equivocation. The verbal tics, rhetorical gestures, and structural habits of academic writing are conventions: we've learned to do them because they signal our participation in a community of professionals and are designed to impart a sense of erudition. But they also produce an epistemological position: a subject of a certain economic class, at least aspirationally so. And these conventions contribute to the impression of a subject apparently outside of the stream of history—outside of its urgencies and its hopes. A subject with minimal attachments, reservedly parsing the options, the data, the arguments. A subject that organizes time without being disoriented by it.

Rationalist discursive styles are not just occasionally stultifying or unsatisfying. This set of tightly orchestrated genres, with little room for variance, associated with most academic work carries a racialized disciplinary force that determines what work, and who, gets read, cited, understood. It determines who enters intellectual history, and for what. Barbara Christian's "The Race for Theory" observed this thirty-five years ago, during the swell of poststructuralism, regarding the canon of largely white writers that had become synonymous with theory, and regarding what work counts as theory at all. As a literary critic, she had been asked continually about a black feminist "method" for reading. She argues against such monolithic systematization and prescription in favor of being changed by each work we read and cultivating a "tuned sensitivity to that which is alive."[21] Christian ends her piece quoting Audre Lorde's "Poetry Is Not a Luxury," which finds in lyrical language a capacity for making the radically new or the frightening *bearable*—an incipient possibility allowed through the dreamlike logics of lyricism, and felt into reality. By now, black feminist theory is fully and distinctly a project characterized by beauty and expressiveness, as well as by writing that averts compartmentalization into theory/practice, academic/popular, as Jennifer C. Nash has shown.[22] Yet even with the institutionalization of black feminist critiques of the norms of academic writing, a formalized rationalism—particularly in historical fields—is the universal parlance, if not the only truly acceptable epistemology.

The dominance of rationalist discursive styles is tied to the "hegemony of Reason" as La Marr Jurelle Bruce names it, modernity's colonialist, ableist, antiblack episteme, which claims "to uphold objective 'truth' while mapping and mastering the world."[23] Bruce's description of Enlightenment's noxious romance with Reason provides the context for his exploration of "black madness," forms of creativity and expression that register to an antiblack world as pathological, angry, or simply "crazy."[24] Bruce writes (gorgeously, sympathetically) about a range of mad black figures, both real and fictional people, Sun Ra and Lauryn Hill, Nina Simone and Eva Canada from the novel

*Eva's Man* by Gayl Jones, Dave Chappelle and Bigger Thomas from Richard Wright's novel *Native Son*. His book lives out a "mad methodology that neither vilifies the madperson as evil incarnate, nor romanticizes the madperson as resistance personified, nor patronizes the madperson as helpless ward awaiting aid. Rather, mad methodology engages the complexity and variability of mad subjects."[25]

Bruce's beginning conceit is an image of Michel Foucault's "ship of fools" crossing paths with the slave ship in the oceanic: "where imprisoned madness meets captive blackness in a stifling tightness through a groundless vastness."[26] And his hope is to connect kinds of madness with the black radical tradition, to connect black madness with forms of art, survival, thriving, and the political field. Black madness appears as "content, form, symbol, idiom, aesthetic, existential posture, philosophy, strategy and energy."[27]

One way to understand Bruce's work is that he reveals how black expression, by virtue of being black, is so often pathologized for its apparent unreadability *as* expression. So, too, the legibility of certain forms of expression within academic life are often tied to the legibility of the people who are doing the expressing.[28] The burden of the reproduction of disciplines often falls most heavily on nonnormative and racialized subjects.[29] Consequently, nonnormative and racialized subjects are the first to experience cost and violence when not reproducing disciplinary boundaries, methods, and epistemologies, even while, or maybe because, their very being is seen as a threat to the perfect reproduction of the discipline. Nonnormative and racialized people are, in this familiar institutional logic, best contained within the bounds of diversification, which is, without fail, the pluralization and proliferation of normativity.

Thus, I want this project to push my fields to think harder about the implications of the dominance of rationalist discourses and their associated styles and conventions in academic knowledge production. I do this not so that we can eject rationalism (as if we could), or abandon all traditional academic forms—this book stretches, disturbs academic forms, but does not *disown* them.[30] I do this so that we can come to see that the hyperperformance and defense of rationalism is colonial, racialized, and gendered, too. Indeed, as Donovan Schaefer has shown, "rationalism" itself is deeply imbued with feeling, even as the felt dimensions of rational knowing are so regularly denied.[31] Part of rationalism's arrogance, though, Schaefer points out, is its claim to secularist neutrality, the illusion of overcoming the ways knowing is experienced precisely as being *felt*.[32]

Traditional academic writing style can be, among other things, the physical architecture of that illusion. So I want this book, via a kind of "postsecular style" (as Kate Stanley puts it), to invite us into closer contact with the unequivocally felt bases of our historical knowing.[33] I want it to loosen our grip. Why do we even care to hold on so tightly to such doggedly rationalist styles and conventions, to shore them up, in the face of the varied urgencies enfolding us? This is not a rhetorical question.

### Story and the Tyranny of Realism

Everything is up in the air, all narratives for the moment have been blown open—the statues are falling—all the metrics are off, if only briefly. —DIONNE BRAND, "On Narrative, Reckoning and the Calculus of Living and Dying"

Natalie Loveless asks a version of this question—Why do we hold onto these styles and conventions when things are in collapse?—in her book *How to Make Art at the End of the World: A Manifesto for Research-Creation*. Loveless narrates the relationship between her artistic practices and research-based practices (in her case, theory, art history), both of which she finds life-giving, but the latter of which gets infinitely more credibility and funding, even *within* the arts wing of the academy. Writing in the ambiance of the Anthropocene and other narratives of world-ending, Loveless holds that "the arts have an important and overlooked part to play in this context. They offer modes of sensuous, aesthetic attunement, and work as a conduit to focus attention, elicit public discourse, and shape cultural imaginaries. 'How might the world be organized differently?' is a question that matters urgently, and it is a question that art—particularly art attuned to human and more-than-human social justice—asks in generative and complex ways."[34] Her hope for research-creation is "curiosity-driven," and "imagines new literacies," "pushing us to tell new stories in the academy, stories that denaturalize singular disciplinary locations while nomadically claiming space within all of them...."[35]

Loveless's manifesto envisions forms of making that alight across and challenge disciplines, and, importantly, "challenge the current hegemony of the book-length monograph," despite her love of the academic monograph.[36] I share both her desire to move between and upset disciplines, and her simultaneous love of and exhaustion with the academic monograph. But I also find her emphasis on *story* enticing. She begins one chapter with a quote from Donna Haraway: "Stories are much bigger than ideologies. In that is our hope."[37]

To claim storytelling as the work of history perhaps sounds simultaneously quaint, obvious, and suspect. Since Hayden White's work, especially *Metahis-*

*tory*, most historians know on some level at least that history is always story and that the realism of history is only an effect of its genre.[38] But there is still an overall reluctance, even refusal, to claim one's own narrativization in historical fields like late antiquity studies.[39] This is even while the study of late antiquity's most famous character, Peter Brown, is a consummate storyteller. Likewise the dominance of ideological critique in biblical studies and, to a lesser extent, religious studies makes anything like an embrace of "storytelling" sound retro or uncritical. So too the use of "storytelling" as a euphemism for brand management and marketing lends it a capitalist pallor. For Loveless, however, who draws from Audre Lorde and Thomas King as well as from Haraway, storytelling is not simply or exactly "narrative." It is about taking the risk of naming a moment with images.[40] It is a mode of carving out more complex realities—an affectively charged and artful mode. It is about redirecting attention, about care for the emergent, as well as ways of refiguring a world already hypersaturated with, founded on, bad stories.

Loveless provokes me to reconsider historical and critical work on antiquity not just as deliberate narrativization, but also potentially as this artful, affectively charged storytelling. We are in a long moment, as Dionne Brand so deftly expressed it, of narrative breakdown. For Brand, the broken story is the credulousness of pre-pandemic "normalcy," speaking itself back into existence with every exhausted sigh of pandemic life.[41] I would add now that the broken story continues to speak with every desire to return to a "before," or to chug along without real recognition of the many kinds of deaths surrounding us. With every concurrent disaster—pandemic, global displacements, systemic collapse, genocide—the brokenness of the story further reveals itself.

This kind of embrace of narrative as imagistic world-making could do more than just move historians and critics into different discursive modes. It could mitigate the tyranny of a certain kind of realism that is the unwritten rule and litmus test of our work: namely, that our renditions must be chastened reproductions, the first effect of which is verisimilitude. Realism is simply a convention of historical work, and not a necessary one.[42] And it is a convention that is, as psychoanalytic theories have amply demonstrated, an elaborate form of fantasy life.[43] More to the point, realism is always a delimiting of the possible; not a description but rather an imposition of a certain kind of "reality."[44] As Sasha-Mae Eccleston observes of the "The Brainsex Paintings" by classicist and poet Anne Carson, in which Carson explores the work of the Greek poet Mimnermos, playing with genre (for instance) can destabilize the realist designs of traditional scholarship. Eccleston writes:

Carson could have relied on the values of realism, scientism, and classical philology, especially because of her scholarly training and the special relationship between Greek literary history and realism. Instead, she draws attention to the variety of methods available for understanding Mimnermos as both poet and person. Carson's approach suggests that this situation is not unique: If we want to grapple with human reality, the elements of fantasy—uncertainty, potentiality, and the sensitivity to the dynamics of perception—that constitute our existence and representations of it should not be excluded. For the stuff of real life is complicated, like working with the fragments of a long-lost poet.[45]

We might think of our work, then, as a way of playing with, framing, renegotiating the real. Images and spun narrative can jar and attune. The embrace of such world-making could also force more of the field to acknowledge the efficacy of things like aesthetics and resonance, the more-than-rational, for making sense of and inhabiting worlds differently. Not only the efficacy of aesthetics and resonance, but the vital, existential importance of them.

So that is why I find myself, in this project even more willfully than other books I've written, engaged in immersive narrativization about the proximity, even occasional indistinguishability, of the long past and the present. Sometimes I produce something that looks like an argument, but more often, I conjure scenes.[46] Historical points emerge, but often through echoes, repetitions, dissonances, and juxtapositions between pieces. I bend translations and make up inscriptions. I speculate. I engage in playful anachronism. There is nothing (of which I'm aware) regulating the points of contact between Christian late antiquity and what is, roughly, "now"—between ancient writers and contemporary figures from my own life, for example. Any intuitive connection was, and is, fair game so long as it felt compelling, alive, or unexpected.

Despite its delinquency with respect to the rules of professionalized historical engagement, I will not relinquish the description of this book as historical. If so much historical work is about defamiliarization, this project, too, defamiliarizes late antiquity, though ironically by rendering it in the hyperfamiliar language of the contemporary world. It defamiliarizes by selecting out details for their beauty or poignancy rather than for their utility in relationship to the usual historicizing categories and schemas: it dilates those details and recalibrates their meanings. The goal is to stretch the boundaries of historical work, and to experiment with historical work as a form of research-creation: to honor artistic forms *as legitimate ways of knowing*, ones which do not need exorbitant attachments to rationalism or realism to hold the specificity of the past as closely as possible, and ones which do not shy from the long past's immanence.

Historical work is frequently about naming continuity and discontinuity with attention and care. We do not need to do that work so rigidly. And while the writing in this book arrives from an excessive and quirky set of reading and observational habits that amount to what we call expertise—expertise that I find generative—expertise is not the *only* place I put my stock.[47] This project places weight on the hope that lyrical knowing can bring relief, expansiveness, and latitude where so many of us have been made clinical, constrained, and numb. And it places the weight on the necessity of metabolizing many times in tandem. As Rukeyser writes, "Who will speak these days, / if not I, / if not you?" This brings me to the question of time and change.

### "It was a period of transformation....": Exceptionalism and Change

For the last fifty years or so, the predominant story of the late ancient Mediterranean has been a story of "transformation." To be sure, there was a lot going on. Roman bureaucracy and elite classes grew, the definition of Roman citizenship broadened, civic administration moved away from the local and became centralized in provincial and imperial structures. Roman rule was increasingly authoritarian, grammar and legal education came to dominate over (and in some cases replace) philosophical education. Associated with Christianity, there was also, of course, the rise in popularity of ascetic behaviors and virtues, of book culture. Monasteries began cropping up from east to west, and shrines for saints peppered cities. In the wake of Christian emperors, over time, traditional Greek, Roman, and indigenous gods and cultic practices (termed "pagan") became controversial, thinned out, got absorbed, or persisted between the lines. People began thinking more in totalizing terms: compendiums, law codes, universal histories.

Peter Brown, whose work essentially reperiodized "late antiquity" and narrated (in particular) Christianity's robust and creative social changes, was central to the popularity of this characterization.[48] To speak of transformation was and continues to be seen as an antidote to the narrative of decline and collapse from Greek and Roman classical culture into the "dark ages," propagated and emblematized in Edward Gibbon's eighteenth-century *The History of the Decline and Fall of the Roman Empire*—although the decline and collapse narrative has hardly disappeared.[49] Importantly, Gibbon's work, steeped in modernist derision for religion, quite notoriously lays the blame for the fall of Rome on Christianity's excesses (as well as on "barbarism").[50] So what has emerged over time in response to the narrative of decline is, as one might guess, a different story not only of the Roman empire, but a different story of Christianity. Christianity was now seen as full of inventive and fascinating (if also sometimes unattractive) characters, new social practices, and expressions of bodily life that were, certainly at first, countercultural within the history of the Mediterranean. Individual subjects, too, were transformed, it seemed, even transforming themselves with this potent new language of Christianity.

But Thomas Hunt's work on "the making of late antiquity" as a field of study has demonstrated just how fully steeped the epistemologies of the field are in the time and space of colonial modernity through its intellectual legacies— its formative figures and scholarship, including Brown.[51] Hunt notes a reliance on not only the French archaeology of colonized Algeria, but approaches to North Africa (and space generally), notions of the human, culture, and civilization very much indebted to the conditions and conversations of French empire and colonization.[52] Thus transformation as creativity/innovation, as a descriptor for late antiquity, carries in it imperialist (and) Christian exceptionalism, I'd argue, even when some of the less savory figures and dimensions of the period or its colonial conditions are being held in view.[53]

It is not only the element of extraordinariness that makes the equation of late antiquity with transformation (unqualified) epistemologically suspect; it is also its implied theory of change. Historical work in general tries to mark and describe change; to name its catalysts and effects. Historians are famous for arguing a case for their geographic and temporal area of expertise as especially fascinating, dynamic, or pivotal. Nonetheless, even leaving aside the problems with periodization, what does it mean to imagine a *particular* period one of "transformation"?[54] How do we gauge the momentousness of change: the number of changes, or the kind (economic, political, social)?

Time and change are fundamentally experiential. They are inescapably tied up in subjectivity and perspective. Some changes are more momentous and resounding in retrospect, some so ephemeral it seems that they hardly happened at all. Some changes are most perceptible to those experiencing them, while in other cases, they are more perceptible to those *not* experiencing them directly. It is difficult to pinpoint change, it requires work and speculation, and in the middle of it we are often hard-pressed to say with any confidence, or at least predict accurately what, exactly, is changing. Change is regularly an experience of uncertainty and disjoint: uncertain in its meaning and scale, disjoint between what is sensed and what is observed.

Time is no less ambiguous. For all of modernism's love of sequential time, for all its confidence in a past entombed and a future that is always not yet, we are constantly navigating asynchronies. So much theorizing of the last few decades has indeed shown how thoroughly multiple temporalities/timelines define power and the management of populations.[55] "The present" is myriad and cacophonous.

Beyond the differential asynchronies that compose the present, though, we live in what Carolyn Dinshaw describes as a present crowded with times and figures that would seem to belong to the long past. In *How Soon Is Now*, Dinshaw describes asynchrony on several levels. She recounts medieval tales of lapsed or jumped time, of belatedness and Rip Van Winkle–style stories, for example, that pepper medieval literature. But she also describes how, contra the linear and developmental temporal conceits of professionalized, modernist historians, amateur readers of medieval literature practice a different relationship to medieval figures and texts, one with its own distinct relationship to temporality. Quite apart from professionalized history, with its regimented schedules and replicable methodologies (not to mention its sometimes chilly disposition), amateur readers tend to work on their own time, or work with the little snatches of time they have found around the edges.[56] Amateur readers additionally lead more overtly with enjoyment: desire and attachment define the work of these readers, as does resourcefulness.[57] In both their offline relationship to the modernist practices of professional history and their grounding in pleasure, Dinshaw argues such amateur readings have a queer force to them. But in this deeply felt relationship to the medieval past, Dinshaw argues that her dilettantes also tend to live closer to the queer asynchronies of the texts they so enjoy.

Readers will see an obvious debt to and kinship with Dinshaw in this book.[58] I share her desire to thoughtfully divest from the relentless performance of strategies and presentations of academic professionalization. I share her recognition that professionalized history has a relationship to modernist (and thus, I would add, colonial/imperialist) time. And I share her sense that the long past was no less full of asynchronies. We know this about late antiquity, specifically, because these asynchronies were often corralled awkwardly and with great labor into grand, monolithic arcs—Julius Africanus's *Chronography* or Eusebius's *Church History*, for example. Likewise we know this because these asynchronies were amplified to fashion and preserve a cultural identity, as in rabbinic literature.[59] We know, too, that fourth-century Christian writers and tourists approached Jerusalem and living Jews as signs and ghosts in their presence of a long-gone past.[60]

With equal debt to Dinshaw and Peter Brown, then, I begin, in the prologue, with that emblematic tale of asynchrony, the Seven Sleepers story. Dinshaw reads this story at length, a story that circulated widely and has had a rich, ongoing life. So the story is a kind of touchpoint between her and Brown—that is, between her queer temporalities and Brown's wistful identification. But while obviously taking cues from both writers, I begin with this story to emphasize a difference in tone and cast. Rather than a tale of miraculous escape and wonder, or of extraordinary large-scale historical transformation, here it is retold as a mundane tale of ambivalent survival, of a desire for a dampened, even deadened consciousness.

This difference in tone and cast enfolds the book, in which the queerness of time is not necessarily or mostly a site or consequence of pleasure, and the historical and personal changes experienced are chilling and deeply uncertain. The figures depicted here are twisted, captivated, frustrated, and undone by time and change. Sometimes their read on *right now* is sweeping and consequential, sometimes they long to lose themselves in a past they never lived, sometimes the future can't come fast enough. They sense change, witness to its losses and possibilities. They crave being architects of their own change and fail to accomplish it. In the middle of it they dream of changeless gods. Change worries and eludes them. They try to finesse the terms of time and change. They do it poorly.

And by *they* I mean *we*, at least many of us, in a tentative and uneasy consortium. One other dimension of the ambiguity of time in this book is not just the proximity, but the blend and bleed between more overtly late ancient figures and contemporary ones, such that those distinctions start to make little sense.

### How We Live in Time

while she waited for something else to happen, she considered that maybe something was happening. —ALEXIS PAULINE GUMBS, *M Archive: After the End of the World*

I have spent a lot of time waiting: waiting to feel better, waiting for things to get better, waiting to see people I love, waiting to find out *what's next*. Feeling trapped in time, drawn thin by it. I have pleaded for change on some days, while on others dreading what particular changes might bring. I'm sure I'm not alone.

Alexis Pauline Gumbs's *M Archive* is a work of speculative documentary that imagines life after the apocalypse into which the present world is living and dying. A collection of lyrical prose pieces that bear out a black feminist metaphysics, Gumbs writes "from and with the perspective of a researcher, a post-scientist sorting artifacts after the end of the world."[61] It honors M. Jacqui Alexander's *Pedagogies of Crossing*, and is written "in collaboration with the survivors, far-into-the-future witnesses to the realities we are making possible or impossible with our present apocalypse."[62] What unfolds across the book is a poetic reinhabiting of a catastrophic world through the language of time and grounded in black life. The present is spoken through the past tense, with the apparently distant future already come, to reveal "a species at the edge of its integrity, on the verge or in the practice of transforming into something beyond the luxuries and limitations of what some call 'the human.'"[63]

So much of *M Archive* is an account of change in all of its gritty particulars, one which knits survival and possibility to conditions of annihilation and neglect. Those who live on develop physical adaptations to their extreme conditions, conditions forged by enslavement and racial capitalism, and these adaptations include sublime new potential and heartbreaking debilitation. Various figures in the book move between being the sinister catalysts of change to physically and psychically overwhelmed subjects whose bodily and environmental changes are beyond their imagination and choice. The changes are somehow both unthinkable to those who undergo them and incredibly quotidian. In this scenario, change is a many-sided thing. Rooted in black ongoingness, "transformation" loses its exceptionalist valences.

I read *M Archive* alongside various pieces of the vast collection of texts of Christian late antiquity—somewhat accidently. I read knowing that Gumbs's imagined but immanent future, a future shaped and propelled by European Christian imperialism and its corollaries, was tied uncannily and irrevocably to the heavy past of Christian late antiquity. It soon began to feel to me as if ancient people also knew somewhere (intuitively, unconsciously) what their strategies and improvisations would become, and were plagued by that intuition.[64] In some cases, I felt that these ancient people were experiencing their losses as beyond them, almost as if they were registering the juggernaut and explosion of colonialist futures of which they were—are—unwittingly a part. I was also sensing uncanny contiguity between some rather unhistorical seeming dimensions of my life and the hyperspecific circumstances of the past. Elements of my world became stories of the long past as it expresses itself in less than predictable ways.[65]

Gumbs's book offers an example of what historian of late antiquity David Maldonado Rivera has argued is the necessity of disobeying the rules of partitioned, linear, colonial time in order to more fully discern the conditions of the world. Maldonado Rivera makes this argument through an account of the way the Catholic church legally retained expropriated property in late eighteenth- and early nineteenth-century Puerto Rico. He describes how juridical reasoning placed the Catholic church in a continuous line with Constantine, thereby producing "the church" as a transhistorical imperial entity. This legal logic, he writes, "turned Puerto Rico into one of the outermost and unlikeliest of territories of a Transatlantic Roman Empire, an eruption of late antiquity into the so-called American Century."[66]

Through this example, Maldonado Rivera points to how critical the organization of time as "linear, unavoidable sentence" is to the ongoing force of colonialism.[67] To counter this colonial temporality, he suggests that historians "cultivate a 'diasporic consciousness' by thinking a historical commons as a tentative connection to the fragments of history rather than the irrefutable certainties of cosmopolitan linear universality."[68] Which is to say normative and colonial histories will not ever be fully undone using normative temporal frameworks. As long as we continue to tell time in the usual ways and with the usual disposition, we will almost inevitably produce the same results, ones that benefit and extend histories of colonialism.

This present book's form, as associatively linked fragments that regularly scramble linear temporality, something like *anachronology*, is in part an attempt to take up Maldonado Rivera's invitation.[69] It is an attempt to create a troubled reckoning with the eerie, diffuse, and unpredictable presence of the past—especially colonial histories which go on in seemingly endless reiteration and territorialize beyond their given historical periods. Gumbs and Maldonado Rivera together compel us to ask generally about ways we might write the "distant past" while experiencing ourselves more fully *in time*. They press us to entertain ourselves as living out—intimately living out—this apparently distant past, and to entertain the distant past as alive in its futures, the futures we now live, futures constantly unfolding. The past is not "finished," in other words, not simply waiting to be uncovered or finally understood.

But if it is true that the past lives expressed in its futures, futures that are constantly in flux, that means that the past is not just pressing on us, not just proximal to us. That means *the past itself is changing*, remaking itself, and only available to us through the crowded now, the edges of which evade us. What would it be to entertain the past not just as fragmentarily alive in its futures, but reorganizing *with* its futures, becoming together with them? Past not as entity, not as what has already passed, but as continuous motion, as passing: passing alongside, in, and through.[70]

## Writing History Differently

What this book is, then, is a post-rationalist, post-realist experiment in living with and writing ancient history differently. The imposition of realism, rationalism, and sequential, developmental time continually racialize academic work and foreclose fuller histories of colonialism, and in doing so they also constrain otherwise historical possibilities. They deny the sensations of time, the disorientations of history. Especially in the face of the international rise of fascism, and the various forms of deadness and numbness that issue from late-capitalist life, it is a matter of spiritual and psychological vitality (or maybe even just *survival*) to be able to think the world and what we call reality outside of its given terms and forms. Fascism and late capitalist commodity culture are nothing if not regimes that reduce (with the hope of elimination) everything outside of the dominant reality *to* the dominant reality.

While I want to make a strong, steady case for the importance of lyricism as an epistemology, my point is not to persuade everyone to write poetry. I am not suggesting myself as a model, at least not in any straightforward way. Rather the point is that this is a parable for writing history differently when it comes to us, as it so often does, in ways we would not choose, and in languages and gestures and styles that are often eccentric to us. The point is to ask what might happen if we took the circumstances of our lives and relationships seriously as conduits for intimate historical knowing even of "distant" pasts. Black feminist theory and writing, as well as affect theory and compatible work in cultural studies, has already framed the realm of subjective experience, intimate relations, mundanity, and the personally felt as a source of historical knowledge about modernity, the present, and the social forces at work in it.[71] But what if ancient forces also appear through a kind of emotional-historical sedimentation? What if, for instance, ancient people's desires are more apprehensible through ours—and ours more elusive because they were never quite ours to begin with?

The point is additionally to encourage ancient historians, in particular, to bring the form of our academic work into more integrity with the shape and texture of our many experiences, proclivities, pains, and creativities.[72] What I'm encouraging is a more conscious proliferation of forms to replace the hollow dogma of canonical discursive academic forms, and a more playful, flexible relationship with those canonical discursive forms without seeing History, itself, as under threat.

But within and through that experiment, this book fashions an ominous and critical re-description—though fragments, figures, and vignettes—of

Christian late antiquity. It does so especially in light of its colonial futures (namely, European modernity and the neocolonial United States), and in the face of many decades of scholarship that has come to think much more generously, to the point of romance, of Christian late antiquity.[73] Both broad and dense, evocative rather than comprehensive, it is something like a postcolonial restyle of Brown's tiny, programmatic, and vivid *The Making of Late Antiquity*.

On a standard timeline, the ancient texts, figures, and scenes appearing in this book would fit between the late second and early third century CE to the sixth century CE, though obviously part of the work of the book is to render that timeline itself a little strange. The book's content is structured by four major and recognizable themes of this period: church fathers, the interior self, the lives of saints, and the so-called decline of paganism.[74] But of course, here too, the collection of material in each of these sections twists and turns and recalibrates the theme.

The first section, "Fathers," launches from late ancient theologians of the early church whose power and influence were growing and changing with the rising status of Christians within the empire. It is a consideration of book culture, intellectual culture, as well as their heavy legacies and menacing political entanglements across time: in other words, intellectuals, power, empire, and writing/paper. These are figures working hard to manage the terms of time and change, and who are, at least sometimes, haunted by that work.

In considering the capacities, real and imagined, endowed in and through writing, I was also preoccupied with the long history of studies of Christian late antiquity and "patristics," the obsessions and disavowed eroticisms (racial/colonial ones, gendered ones) circulating especially around certain scalar and jurisdictional approaches to time and language: the gravitas and spiritualized attachments to the microscopic phenomena of philology, the impulse to periodize and reperiodize, the urge to produce encyclopedic volumes, meticulous commentaries, and exhaustive chronicles. By no coincidence, the approaches to time and language mimic those of the very ecclesial figures I silhouette here.[75]

Threaded through this section, as others, are reflections on my family—in this case especially my father—and their relationship to paper.

The second section ("Notes from the Interior") explores the increasing interest in late antiquity in subjective interiority, and works out the violent and sustaining dimensions of confession and the inner space of the self. I crave a richer, more complicated discussion of interiority than the Foucauldian framework, which locates in late antiquity precedents for later forms of interiorized self-regulation, permits. I aim for this in part by more fully inhabiting the meanings and possibilities of interiority, and by linking psychological/subjective interiority to the increasing obsession in that period with physical virginity—sometimes imagined as an untouched inner space—and to colonial, sexualized violence. Freud's "dark continent" of female sexuality and the racial violence of modern gynecology appear, in this section, as logics both inherited from late ancient writers and living contiguously with them. And especially since biographical fragments of my own appear across the book, it felt necessary to complicate self-narration in this section by placing it in this tweaked history of interiority. What is self-narration after all if not an attempt to control the story of what changed you and how? Augustine, famed writer of the long biographical monologue, the *Confessions*, looms large.

The third section, "Saints' Lives," begins from an understanding of late ancient hagiography as a literature of grief and its abeyance. It describes experiences of durational crisis and unsatisfied desires for transformation and agency under such conditions. Indeed the ascetic practices of spiritualized deprivation modeled by the saints have in so much scholarship been understood as "transformative," and creating a new kind of subjectivity—reproducing some of the language of the ancient literature itself.[76] So it is in this section that I try to mitigate the romance of that narrative, which works as a synecdoche for the "transformation" of Christian late antiquity at large. Saints' lives and the ascetic practices they commend are stories of aggrandizement. What happens when that work of aggrandizement becomes more transparent? This aggrandizing work, and its foundering at covering over the mundane conditions of grief, feels associatively close to Lauren Berlant's work on "slow death" in *Cruel Optimism*. In this section I play out the possibility of ascetic practice as part of the undercurrent and social-emotional landscape of some structures of contemporary life, particularly higher education.[77] As one iteration of a more generalized surfacing of hagiography's unsatisfied desires for agency and transformation, I also play with portraits of women saints in ways that complicate feminist critical recuperations of agency, recuperations which still hold critical sway in the field.

The fourth and final section, "The Passing World," homes in most specifically on loss and history's ephemerality, memory and memorialization. It does so through explorations of some of the corollaries of the eventual Christian dominance of the late ancient landscape and imperial managements of the past. So for example, the changing place of the traditional Greek and Roman gods with the eventual dominance of Christianity across the Roman empire offers a needle's eye into complex, often eroticized attachments to authority, attachments that only become *more* complex when that power and authority wanes. In a series of fabricated inscriptions, for example, I write through the metaphor of one's god losing influence, or being in some sense gone, as a way of getting at structural change, and the strange, slippery work of trying to document the erosion of formative relationships—or loss at all. This section also contemplates the nostalgia and attachments of an invented classicism of this period, as well as Christian colonization of Jewish history. Overall, this section most pointedly houses meditations on the vague and distorting nature of change, as well as meditations on power: delicate and multifaceted bonds with it, and then the hollow anticlimax of tentatively securing it.

In each part and across sections, other networked themes emerge. Some of those themes: Gardens. Mirrors. Goldenness. The ocean. Exhaustion. On a grand scale, the crushing experiences and constant perils of living in late capitalist imperialism—which is shaped by Christian strategies and conceptualities in ways both more subtle and more forceful than one might think. Throughout, I pose the question: what if ancient Christians' strategies and hopes and rejoinders did not succeed for them in the way they, and we, imagined? Or rather, *what if they are succeeding, in an extant way, and to disastrous ends?*

Read this book laterally, not literally. Read it for proximal and residual effects. Read it for passing impressions, for the grain and quality of relations. Read it as a passage out of which both past and present emerge ever more distinctly, emerge remade.

# Prologue

### I Wish I Was One of the Seven Sleepers of Ephesus

I have been that tired. So tired that I could pass out for two hundred years. So tired that my only speech was to God, Please just let me sleep. Paramedics enter the house across the street, the low red light flashing over the arterial blues of January. It's too early for tragedy, for more of it. What I wouldn't do to hide from all of this, the constant emergency, just outside the house. To let the centuries pass in a cave, wearing the same clothes day after day, blank but unscathed through the racket, the houses razed. Emperors and gods would rise and recede, famines would bloom and fade. And then one day I'd rouse to a sky no longer flurried with the ash of burning flesh, and suddenly the cross, the mark of my survival, is everywhere looming.

## Sleeping Through It

In *Anaesthetics of Existence*, Cressida Heyes describes a set of experiences that do not quite qualify as experiences. Or, at least, they test the limits of what we tend to think of as "experience." Medical sedation, chemical inebriation (recreational drugs, alcohol), unconsciousness, sleep. These conditions, ones on the "edges" of experience, are potent ones. Ones that take on new meanings (and sometimes unusual appeal) under the conditions of late capitalism. In an approach at once phenomenological and genealogical, Heyes describes for instance the cultural "desire for the anaesthetic, the withdrawal from sensory experience, as a mode of managing pleasure and pain" in order to deal with the large-scale sensory overload of modernity.[1] Drawing on Susan Buck-Morss, she notes how "the aesthetic shock of modernity coincides with the development of technologies of anesthesia":

> Opiates, nitrous oxide, ether, chloroform, and cocaine entered widespread everyday use through the 1800's (Snow 2006), developing their own economy (both within and outside formal medical practice) as varied tools for coping with synaesethetic overload. No longer dependent on anesthetic habits as quaint as daily laudanum or ether frolics, we now have an amazing array of drugs aimed at managing the ubiquitous depression, anxiety, insomnia, and other synesthetic diseases that thrive in contemporary Western cultures.[2]

In one chapter called "anaesthetic time," Heyes thinks about everyday, largely bourgeois, substances like wine and cannabis, that can "take a while to consume, or have slow, drawn out, and relatively mild effects on one's sensorium, and provide a way of checking out of any metaconciousness of time's passing moments."[3] She notes that "time drifts" while or after taking these drugs. "Instead of the linearity of a punctuated time, a time divided into ever smaller units, each of which must be productively used, they induce a relative indifference to time passing and to the sensory demands that render our typical temporality so exhausting."[4] She compares the work of these substances to the way junk food functions in Lauren Berlant's theorizing of "slow death," as an interruption and suspension of trajectories toward health and future.[5] And Heyes argues that these substances generate "a different lived experience of time. It moves on without our noticing—whether because we are sitting in a haze, numb, or because, more literally, we're unconscious (blacked out, sedated, asleep)."[6] This anaesthetic time is a logical response to the incessant demands on our attention and time, "a way of surviving an economy that is relentlessly depleting."[7]

Heyes also discusses sleep: that mundane, universal condition of not doing, or un-doing. It is one in which we relinquish our will and our watchfulness. In other words, in this condition "our lived experience fails to line up with the qualities of an autonomous subject."[8] Anaesthetic time, as including sleep or similar forms of unconsciousness, is "an experiential encounter with complete withdrawal from the exhaustion of contemporary fantasies of autonomy...." What's more, in an economic and political environment in which one's self and life are endless projects of effort and cultivation, "the pressures of self-making generate their own demand for respite, for a retreat to a space undefined by working on the self."[9]

*Maybe they were very tired.*

The story of the seven sleepers of Ephesus can be found in Gregory of Tours, a sixth-century Roman historian from Gaul, though it has an extensive life beyond then—and possibly before it was about Christians in a changing empire.[10] It is, in any version, a story about change. But in this version, the changes are several: the story begins with the brothers having changed their mind about worshipping the "lifeless images" of the traditional gods. They feel remorse, and are baptized, upon which their names, too, are changed. Decius arrives in Ephesus and demands that Christians be found and burned. Under a sky dark with smoke and the ash of victims, the brothers pray to their god to intervene. They are found and brought before the emperor in a scene reminiscent of martyr stories, where they refuse to sacrifice to their old gods, even despite the danger. They *remain unchanged*, in other words. But the emperor, instead of killing them on the spot, releases them for no apparent reason other than that they are young and beautiful (that one of them was a magistrate's son probably didn't hurt, either). The brothers go into hiding in a cave and fall asleep, where they are sealed up at the emperor's order, only to be found by a shepherd ages later. God ordered the spirits be returned to their bodies, and they awoke strong and gorgeous as they were before, not even their clothes showing signs of age. The only thing that had changed was the world.

Gregory's telling of the story hints at a desire for a Christian subject who is, so to speak, out of his time: one who is wildly at odds with dominant culture and imperial authorities. Whether this kind of Christian ever existed is anyone's guess. The more interesting question is what this kind of imagination of Christians would do for people living in and with Christian imperialism. What is it to tell a miraculous story of survival in which one is unscathed by time and political change? Or, to turn it another way, what is it to tell a miraculous story in which you are asleep to your own power and collusion?

The Seven Sleepers is more than a story about social change. The Seven Sleepers is a story about anaesthetic time—not only portending and anticipating it, but remade by it. The story is a wish to sleep through the demands and turmoil of living, through the boredom of waiting for change. A wish to pull the cord from an unyielding, if latent, awareness. Wanting an interruption of the relentlessness of the present is understandable. But this story suggests that the long sleep of anaesthetic time is also sometimes or simultaneously a more ambivalent wish to live on without being marred by witness: to be relieved of even that most minor intercession. To simply wake up, well-rested, secure, vital as ever, under a translucent sky, hardly recalling a thing.

PART I

¤ \ ¤ / ¤

# Fathers

*

"This Christian view was comprehensive in two senses of the word: *totalizing*, seeking to gather together all that existed into clear and definable intellectual categories; and *knowing*, seeking to create a cognitive mastery of all that existed in the Christian world."[1]

[There is the writing that comes from an appetite for command. Then there is the writing that comes from a sense of debilitation. The problem is that it is often hard to tell the difference.]

## Chronography, in Fragments (with Julius Africanus)

### 1

I spread it all before me
like animal viscera or tarot
or puzzle pieces in dim
light, the events
in all their miscellany meanings,
the past that silent oracle.

### 2

Understand, my life made no sense.
I began to stitch everything
into that fabric, chemical formulas,
acts of war, hair from my sister's brush,
the only poor history
a partial one.

### 3

The moon spoke cryptically
a slow story of depletion.
Lord let me have one
thing whole, and lord,
let it be everything.

## Eusebius Tries to Organize Time, Part I

I'll begin from no other place than God's plan for history. —EUSEBIUS OF CAESAREA, *The History of the Church*

Lost in the soft obscurity of trees, he craved forest. And then when the forest wasn't enough, he craved the cosmos. And then nothing less than the cosmos in its singularity, the world's episodic fragments crystallized into the hard elegance of a line. The calamity of empires transposed into the cool tranquility of a table.

How else to describe the monument of right now, glaring and operatic, but with the cumulative weight of everything that came before? Every era truncated and leaning, shouldering forward, driving to disclose its final meaning *in time*. Disparate geographies bound together *in time*, hostages to synchrony.

He imagined himself the master of ceremonies, or better, the conductor: each small gesture pulling strings tied to the arms of musicians, the sound rising like water before a countless crowd. His special power was to exhume one note, vibrating and strange, from the gut of every living thing. To hear the same pinging everywhere. It was the only true way to celebrate a god so unrelenting, an eternity of arrows.

\*

"[A. H. M.] Jones prided himself on using the earliest editions of the sources, sometimes from the 17th or 18th century, and his skill at translating, absorbing and interpreting Greek and Latin texts was honed during more than a decade of rigorous training in the classics, first at Cheltenham and then at New College. He was able to transmit to paper his familiarity with the original texts as easily as he was able to bring it to bear in debates with colleagues or in seminars with his students. . . .

"Jones' mastery of the primary sources and the languages in which they were written in turn formed the basis of a dogmatic adherence to 'authentication,' which became increasingly obsessive later in life. In short, Jones' long experience of studying the classics imbued him with a *reverence* for original texts, which he felt should lie at the heart of all historical writing. It seemed to me the only point he imposed on his students."[2]

## The Weight of Paper, I

For this reason Jesus appeared. He took that book on as his own. He published that edict of the Father on the cross. What glorious teaching. —*Gospel of Truth*

The books were very heavy. Like watermelons in your arms. At first, though, books were rare: there were scrolls, papyrus, parchment. But not yet books. Binding came later, along with the need to compile. The need to compile because there was so much to sort through. So many letters, pamphlets, accounts, receipts. So many laws scrawled down in an improvisation of justice far from any emperor's eye. Predictably the books became unwieldy. The books would need to be very large. Multi-volume. Endless.

Books and paper also had exalted status. Almost cosmic. Especially in a time and place in which hardly anyone could read. To have something written down was mystique, with the potential for certitude or deceit. How to know what could be trusted, what with all of those documents changing hands, floating around? And the more writing there was the more each word demanded adjudication: trickery or truth? Meanings mushroomed. So too the professionals who concocted them, self-serious arbiters of verity, grew with the books. In stature and number. Ballooned to exorbitant size.

Early in the life of the ballooning book: Origen of Alexandria. Writing in the early third century, enviably prolific, an allegorical reader whose devotion to Christ as Word materialized, surprisingly literally, in a career of words. He wrote endlessly, but his work was sorting: the Hexapla, for instance, a critical edition of the Hebrew Bible rendered in six horizontal columns. This kind of sorting was, however, not enough. Readers and readings themselves had to be sorted—into fleshly, soulful, and spiritual. The spiritual readers understood the Word to not be about letters and sounds but about transformative knowledge:

> Resolve to learn in you there is the capacity to be transformed, and to put off the form of swine, which is an impure soul, and the shape of a dog, which is that of a man who barks and reviles and pours out abuse.... Let us learn from the apostle that the transformation depends on us. For he says this: "We all, when with unveiled face we reflect the glory of the Lord, are transformed into the same image." If you are like a barking dog, and if the Word has moulded and transformed you, you have been transformed from being a dog into being a man. If you were impure and the Word came to your soul and you submitted

yourself to the moulding of the Word, you changed from being a swine to being a man. (Origen, *Dialogue with Heracleides*)[3]

But the truth of a text beyond the literal—the spiritual meaning—was not effortless. It did not rise off the text like steam off tea. It had to be procured. *Effected*. It was a matter of exposure and extraction. It was a matter of the textual expert "unveiling" what was behind the bare letter, the scene of interpretation morphing into a scene of forced and eroticized exhibition.[4] It was also a scene of torture: the bent body of the text held down, yielding whatever it can, whatever it must.[5] The transformation of the words echoed the tortured transformation of the Word.[6] Which was heavier, the book or its reader?

Born in Egypt, named for an Egyptian god, but offered all the bells and whistles of Greek education in Alexandria, it is not clear how Egyptian Origen imagined himself to be.[7] To be Alexandrian never quite had the racial taint of "Egyptian."[8] There is a hint, maybe, in his reading of the biblical stories of Israel's plundering of Egypt's treasure: having a little Egypt is okay, but too much becomes a hazard, a pollution.[9] And Origen wrote—voluminously—before an imperial Christianity: in the low thunder of state violence, a violence he (and others) aggrandized as martyrdom. He also wrote, for part of his life, from colonial Palestine, where he argued with Jews on the interpretation of their own scriptures.[10] What he desired was legitimacy, authentication: In *Against Celsus*, he speaks in his familiar key of philosophy to make a plea to a Platonist philosopher that Christian wisdom is the loftiest of "barbarian"—that is, foreign—wisdoms.

Celsus was dead. Origen argued, in their shared language, with a long-dead Platonist philosopher, whose disparagements apparently rung in his ears, hoping mainly to be seen as part of a people who were civilized. Or at least *more* civilized than the lawless, godless masses of other foreigners who offered nothing.[11] Why answer after a hundred years? To sort through the mess, and to sew up the unfinished business of Celsus's shoddy readings of Christian texts. To iron it all out, and to wring out what he could from those texts, and ascend, at least in his imagination, through the vast echelons of the uncouth and deliver *knowledge*. To deliver something pristine, true.

His allegorical interpretation, then, was the kind of elevation to higher being that was at once promised and foreclosed by the social and racializing hierarchies that so pervaded ancient thinking.[12] The climb was endless, and there was always someone to supersede you.

Celsus, we can imagine, would have been unmoved by Origen's prolix rejoinder. But Origen desired legitimacy, and legitimacy he got, for both

Christian wisdom and himself. He was a source of exegetical imitation, of inspiration for his translation, and for his tabular organization of knowledge—and later, a source of angst, as the Christian bishop Epiphanius placed him (and those associated with him) again *almost* ironically in a category no less defined by foreignness: heresy.

Before all that, though, Origen's story is a story of books and writing and wanting to be *more*. An imagination that reading the right things and reading the right way could bootstrap you up into some other state, or at least prevent you from plummeting. It was a desperate hope, an obsessive one, weighed down, perhaps, by the rotten knowledge of what contrived gymnastics it is to wrench yourself upward, and how iffy your state is even then; or perhaps weighted by worry about how strenuous it is to hold a body and keep it down. And how jumbled its words, when spoken.

## The Grammarians

*...the sense that grammatical work salvages what it can from disaster....* —CATHERINE MICHAEL CHIN, *Grammar and Christianity in the Late Roman World*

It is a very particular kind of love,
to break something down
into parts. To love each piece
is to love more, to have more
to love, and that's what it was, love—
to get lost in a text and its secret orders,
to draw out worlds from words: the line, the list,
the concatenations of time
like a thread unspooled.

We loved hard.
We read in the original languages.
Spoke of nothing
but the lacquered past.

Outside there was only suffering.
I remember hearing
there was suffering. The trials
and frenzy of living. Words worn down
to muted sounds. People languished,
dead language.
While here inside the manor
of the lord of erudition, we read more.
We parsed verbs. We stayed close
to the text.

[That volume of writing can be its own kind of negation.]

### Jerome, Apology

I did not know how to be alone. These books were my comfort, the words, these women—so captured by my letters, they recited them by heart. How then could I stop?

## Jerome, Apology

You see, I have actually been to all of these places. I learned the languages perfectly. I was in the sun so long my skin became like an Ethiopian boy.

Jerome, Apology

I only asked her to read to me.

## The Weight of Paper, II

If any fields on a form are left blank, it will automatically be rejected. Even if it makes no sense for the applicant to fill out that field. For example, if 'Apt. Number' is left blank because the immigrant lives in a house: rejected. Or if the field for a middle name is left blank because no middle name exists: rejected, too. It's not clear what problem this new policy was intended to solve. In response to a detailed list of questions about the purpose behind the processing change, U.S. Citizenship and Immigration Services (USCIS) sent only a vague statement saying applicants "must provide the specific information requested and answer all the questions asked." —CATHERINE RAMPELL, "The Trump Administration's Kafkaesque New Way to Thwart Visa Applications"

Roman law, as a locally distributed bureaucratic system, was a long and elaborate series of attempts to manage its vast and cumbersome constituency. To name and capture their affiliations, prerogatives, and positions—often moving ones: "Ancient legal systems in general, and Roman law in particular, devoted immense energy to the classification of persons and the distribution of rights, duties, agency, and disabilities at law."[13]

This generated a lot of paper. The problem is that paper, in great volumes, was hard to manage. Roman bureaucracy became, over time, ever more like its population: a vast and cumbersome project. It ran roughshod over the very peoples it hoped to systematize. A. H. M. Jones first chronicled this at length in his nearly as vast and cumbersome three-volume 1964 epic, *The Later Roman Empire*.[14] For Jones, Roman administration was hasty but not efficient. In a stretch when emperors and administrators were in constant flux, the empire relied increasingly on offices rather than individuals for continuity—offices as placeholders that gives the impression of structure, of consistency. Legal petitions had allure for the promise of justice, but often went unheard or shoddily addressed and bowed, as always, in the direction of the rich. Roman administration was a rusty machine, and it was a paper machine, generating more documentation than it could digest.[15]

Jones's picture is one of "sclerotic chaos," as Peter Heather describes it, a picture which was drawn up with some comparative reference to Jones's own (clearly ambivalent) bureaucratic experiences in the British Ministries of Labour and National Service and Military Intelligence during World War II.[16] Roman administration in all its clumsiness, Heather seems to suggest, could not imagine such precision and reach.

But the unwieldiness of documentation, its sheer volume and incoherence, is part of documentation's power. Labyrinthine and full of incongruities, the collection of laws of the early fourth-century Theodosian code, for instance, housed such an enormously long and wide legal history that it thwarted any single cogent legal position: "The very nature of the Code and its arrangement made any reading uncertain."[17] This was to the benefit of emperors, who could exploit the fogginess of the very mass effort at documentation they had encouraged: "In such a capricious and ever-changing world, only emperors themselves could grant a greater degree of assurance. Certainty depended on them alone—and even that remained unsure."[18] Unsure because the whims of emperors were as capricious as anything else.

British bureaucratic practices had been a long-running practice of colonial population management in Jones's time, the consequences of which continue. They reverberate, as Yael Berda shows, in postcolonial states whose independence has been won (India), for instance, and the management of captivity in colonized Palestine. She writes: "The colonial state catalogued people according to their relationship to the government: from loyal citizens, collaborators, and cooperators to subjects, enemies, and those of doubtful loyalty. These were not only used as counterinsurgency measures to quash uprisings or strikes but were central in the administration of the everyday, particularly the applications for identity documents that enabled movement."[19]

Empire operates through endless forms of inclusion and exclusion: inclusion into empire's juridical and taxonomic reach, and exclusion from its highest privileges.[20] Borders after all are never, even now, about geography; not about protecting a presumably discrete inside. They are about managing and extracting resources, authorizing and constraining mobility.[21] They are about the differential distribution of vulnerability. Essential to this is the cataloguing of stratified difference.

An object lesson in how to catalogue difference: half a century earlier than the Theodosian code, but similarly ambitious and incoherent, was Epiphanius of Cyprus's *Medicine Chest*, or "Cure-all." It was a comprehensive compendium, though not one of laws—one of eighty heresies.[22] It was a work at once ethnographic and fantastical. Fantastical *because* ethnographic: it was drawn up with the familiar form of characterizing foreign peoples, their origins, and their qualities, in flamboyant and slanderous ways.[23] This included their "bad piety."[24] He was a collector and indexer of diversions from the norm, of defectors from truth, of queasy thinkers who needed correction.

For Epiphanius, the cosmos from its earliest glimmerings was a long story of error. From Adam to Babel to the golden calf and the idols of the Greeks: it was all error, error that must be tracked. Error that must be rectified. It was a *Medicine Chest* because it was tonic for the poison of the apparent outside, an outside that nonetheless fascinated him, or at least fascinated him enough to write three lengthy volumes.

But the outside was no longer outside, simply by virtue of its place in Epiphanius's schema: "the foreign" was always within his vast universe, ready to be managed.[25] And whatever the supposed heresies themselves meant to the readers of this popular work, surely something else resonated: the safety and force of the classification of difference. Name it. Put it all down. Put it on paper. Mark the errors. Make sure there's nothing missing.

### Jerome, Translating

Take note. This is the art of transposition: to capture without killing. To take a verse and strip it down. Peeling inflection. To scour and clutch it, then feel its beating heart alive in your hands.

## Eusebius Tries to Organize Time, Part II

He dreamed of branches crashing through his roof, woke to the sound of breaking glass. Panicked, he went to the sea. He stood for days at the edge of the shore, the line that wasn't one, harrowed by the water's endless erasures. Nothing moved forward that didn't pull back, eroding even him.

Having read that order overrode all of this, he reassured himself that history couldn't begin here, in this place without beginnings, this vastness without words, a chaos no true god would ordain.

## The Weight of Paper III

Paper, in great volumes, was hard to manage. Think of the weight: cartons of envelopes, for example, pressed out by machines.

Machines were staples of my childhood landscape, although I never thought about them. I was born in Bethlehem, Pennsylvania, the location of an old Moravian settlement, called later "the Christmas city." It was also a city of industrial ruins: Bethlehem Steel had one of the largest mass layoffs of its time, on "black Friday," the year before I was born. So in Bethlehem, in the same sightline as the old brick churches and stone streets and the many-pointed Moravian star on the hill, visible for miles, was a hulking, discontinued steel plant.

My grandparents' house, twenty minutes from there, was a tiny Levittown house with linoleum floors and a pantry that was my father's old bedroom. It had all the trappings of a working-class Catholic home—the refrigerator packed with kielbasa and cut watermelon and cantaloupe, the mass-produced statues of Mary the mother of Jesus and disembodied praying hands, the generosity and arguments punctuated with cracks of laughter. The air conditioner ran from May to September in a dutiful hum.

My dad and both of his parents worked with or around heavy machines all of their lives. My grandpop worked in construction until he retired, one effect of which was tinnitus so distracting that he could only fall asleep with the TV on at high volume. My gram worked in factories for forty years. Her first and then her last job both involved paper. The first, when she was fourteen, at a cigar factory, after her mother died. The last, at Boise Cascade, or what became MailWell, for two decades where she produced mailer advertisements. Advertisements for AARP benefits or magazine subscriptions. The kind of thing you threw right in the trash, or later, the recycling bin. Forty hours a week filling large cardboard boxes with mailer advertisements and envelopes. All that I knew about this was that she would bring home large cardboard boxes for me and my sister to make a house. To draw on with fat crayons or the fruited toxicity of permanent markers. Windows stabbed out with my grandpop's box cutter.

But her labor appeared in other ways. She opened and read every piece of mail delivered to their house no matter how irrelevant. "There is no such thing as junk mail," she said. There was also the arthritis from the physical labor, so bad her back curved and her knuckles were inflamed knobs. She spent the last twenty years or more taking excessive amounts of Oxycontin, probably addicted, to deal with the pain and, I imagine, also the childhood trauma.

My dad spent his life working in waste management and what was at the time a budding environmental industry. Later in his career, he worked in recycling. He started a business that repurposed construction waste. He did this with little conscious connection to his parents and their labor.

I suppose I elevated the family work with paper, with waste: I study texts found in ancient trash piles, and the mass-produced Bible. I reread old texts, recycle them, make them continually reusable. Rescue them from decomposition. I write books. I treasure paper in an increasingly paperless world. "Physical books are irrelevant," I'm told. This is what I love. I love books because I can hold them, feel them heavy in my hands.

## Apophasis

I inherited my father's philosophy of heartbreak, his doctrine of reverence for ordinary hours: the grassy morning, the loose heat of the summer's late afternoon, the many grays of the cemetery at night. Behind him a music played, all bittersweet chords.

We'd walk for hours after dinner, the dogs barking at us from their yards. His teachings, which he could not truly say, became my work to render, a career of transcription. His grief became mine. His loves, also mine.

Now, banging on the windows of a sterile, impassive Spring, I remember our sour cherry tree's last gasp, the barest pink bloom after so many years of nothing. My father piled cherries into plastic soup containers, the whole neighborhood ate them. I could write a hundred books. What could be in them? Not that, not him.

# Interlude

## On the Origin of the World

It was a terrible birth:
preeclamptic, lost fluids and tissue draining on the green paper napkins.
No one was ready, monitors and drugs barely plugged in, the stainless
 steel
besting her body's own ruthlessness. The child forcing their way out
like a swear word, ready to suck the air. Was it even a child, this creature,
 sticky
and pale, still reeking of innards; or a shadow of something else, another
 time
come to live, without invitation, tearing into this time, a time of pain
and pain management, organs emptied, the drying of cold sweat?

Who will love you, one untimely born, your recalcitrant presence,
still half-baked and poorly conceived? No one asked for you and there
you were, wet as if pulled from the deep, where there was not light,
only the reflection of light, the imitation of stars.[1]

PART II

¤ \ ¤ / ¤

# Notes from the Interior

\*

"The idea that God could search the heart was central to the Christian sensibility of the age.... The greatest gift God might give to men placed in a special relationship with Him was the gift of His all-seeing eye to peer into the hearts of men...."[1]

\*

"Roman literature shows us repeatedly how the interior refuge in the imperial imagination functions both as nostalgic utopia and as the intoxicating space of security-as-horror."[2]

[At some point there was nowhere else left to go except deeper and deeper inside.]

## Prudentius Considering Dawn

> Soon likewise our darkness
> and the heart conscious of its sin
> will clear when the clouds disperse,
> and grow light, when God rules.
> —PRUDENTIUS, *Morning Hymn*, trans. O'Daly

I couldn't decipher what was inside and what was outside of me.
All of it was obscurity. This is what it is to be lost in your own metaphor,
sitting at your perch, scouring the sky for daybreak, owl-like, depraved.

What is Christ if not relief from yourself, a harsh clarity
blaring through fog? This is what I waited for: Christ like a spear,
ripping the night, waited to be like Jacob rescued from wrestling

and restlessness by dawn, sapped and taken out, but still seeing the face of God
in the morning. It is sickness to bisect the world. The eradication of clouds.
I wanted to believe that I too could be light. But I was the night, I was the spear.

## Augustine, Confessing (a thread)

Let me first say that I do not condone theft of any kind
but it was stealing that brought me the greatest pleasure.
I was the wide-grinning prince of minor transgressions 1/

learning first all of the wrong lessons, and held in place
by the bodies I touched; organized, crystallized by the
frenzied current of sex in bad faith. In other words 2/

I have lived poorly. I was a cyclone with no center,
undulating spoliation, running in any weather, but
unable to escape the sensation, like a bad taste in the mouth, 3/

of needing redemption. I spent years of my life
drowning in my own ambivalence, hacking away
at that frozen lake to see how cold it gets 4/

at the bottom. I don't know who needs to hear this but
you too can be good. It is only a matter of time before you
end up alone, ruddy and wretched from crying, in self-imposed 5/

exile at the park, staring down to the river moving
at the pace of your desperation. Something save me from this,
you will think, finally, and this time you mean it, and like 6/

the slow drift of a child's singing, that something
will arrive. I say this here because there is no finer balm
for the unsettled soul than to detail each blazing injury 7/

and what is any petty revelation without its public, what
sound is more ethereal, what cause more virtuous
than your own voice, drunk with catharsis, speaking itself 8/

into emptiness, flush with the rewards of reaching out,
not just for God, but for this genre.

## Augustine's Mirror

Augustine's life, or at least his rendition of his life, was one long speech to God. As if in calling out to God his life got called up too,[3] a fishhook to his viscera. Each petition a little golden shovel nicking the dirt, until hours later he was up to his hips in a narrow hole, hitting no bottom, only more earth, where even leaves and bones are pestled grit.

Augustine's god was a god far beyond Augustine yet somehow, eerily, also a god that lived in Augustine's memory, that had insinuated godself among his memories, with colors, with music, with the taste of pears. It was a shadowy museum, Augustine's mind, where objects and gods lived, forgotten, until the little bell, or until someone comes calling. The recesses of it disturbed him:

> For you, Lord, judge me, because although no one can know a person's thoughts, except their own spirit within them, there are some things which even their own spirit doesn't know. But you, Lord, know all there is to know of them because you made them. Although in your sight I despise myself and consider myself dust and ashes, there is one thing that I know about you which I do not know about myself. I know that it is impossible for you to be harmed, whereas I do not know which temptations I can resist and which I cannot. (*Confessions* 10.5)[4]

He would confess, he concluded, both what he knows and what he doesn't know. He would confess from the soil, confess from the hall of the shadowy museum: "This much I know, although right now, 'I see in a mirror dimly, not yet face to face,' . . ."[5] He worshipped a god who promised transparency, who promised more than the mirror did with its fog and its fault. Curious then to find, in other places in Augustine, the mirror could still promise a lot: "God held up his scripture to you, a mirror [*speculum*] for you . . . see if you are what is said," he writes.[6] With its endless capacity to produce commentary, especially in Augustine's time, clarity is perhaps not scripture's hallmark.[7] Ironically, it was indeed scripture—first Corinthians—he quoted on the mirror's dimness.

In other writings of Augustine, too, words act as mirrors—even his own words had his readers seeing uncannily themselves.[8] But *these* words seem to shoot back with silvered optimism a self-understanding that the confessing Augustine cannot get. In the *Confessions*, Augustine's words, spoken to God and himself and, slyly, to a readership he occasionally acknowledges, only lead further down the rabbit hole. Transparency eludes him even with ostensibly undimmed scripture constellating his speech, speaking to and with and for him. What scripture says is that there is only self-knowledge *in the future*. And so he looks there with trust, and toward a god of cut glass, even as another god watched: the one who furnished the fishhook, the shovel, and whose silence brought forth from the hazy surface, depth.

### Interior: House

When you pray, pray
from the depths, from the bottom
of the house, from the basement

with the plywood door. Pray from captivity. Pray
face down, seeing from the corner of your eye
the Philadelphia Eagles poster reflected in the mirror.

Pray to the person, the parent, above you,
upstairs, the floorboards bending and creaking
under them. You can hear

them but they cannot hear you, an inversion
of every theology. What noise could you make
anyway against this gangly earthly power?

Give thanks for the great mercy
of blacking out, for the last precious
minutes when you could feel your body

as your body, when on the late drive
home from his underground room,
gripping the wheel, exiting yourself,

you could for one final time smell
your own summer skin. It will take
decades to remember gentleness, he will

forever know more than you, the stark
omniscience of a teenage boy, a man
somewhere now, his old room

no doubt a place of comfort,
of privacy
for him who broke you.

Pray, if you can,
from there.

[I have often fantasized about what it was like inside his head.]

## Dark Continents

"We need not be abashed on this account; the sexual life of grown-up women, too, is still a 'dark continent' for psychology...." Sigmund Freud writes in "The Question of Lay Analysis" (1926), registering his ongoing frustration with the obscurities of women's sexuality.[9] He flips this metaphor out like a coin onto a table. It spins and falls.

The coin is borrowed. He lifts it from Welsh adventurer Henry Morton Stanley, Ranjana Khanna notes, whose expeditions to Africa aided and abetted the nineteenth-century mapping and colonization of central Africa.[10] Khanna finds kinship across Freud and Stanley's writings, since Stanley's tales of his travels are beset with "deep anxieties about women,"[11] and Freud imagined women's sexuality as containing traces of an "undeveloped," primordial phase, one preceding civilization.[12] So while Freud more distinctly speaks of gender and sexuality, and Stanley more distinctly of racialized territory, in both cases, the metaphor conjures eroticized, racialized space. Stanley and Freud not only both understand their work as forms of adventure and expedition, Khanna shows, they also find their thinking shaped by *archaeology*. For instance, they both evoke the ruins and remains of Pompeii as an analogy for the recesses of personal history.[13] The objects of memory are buried in dirt and ash: "Forty years of my life has passed, and this delving into my earliest years appears to me like an exhumation of Pompeii...."[14]

We might say they were both preoccupied with depth: the spatialization of obscurity. Geography personalized. The interior as that which cannot be seen but (apparently) invites insinuation. Interiority appears repeatedly in Stanley's *Through the Dark Continent* (1878). It is where Stanley begins:

> I thus became possessed of over one hundred and thirty books upon Africa, which I studied with the zeal of one who had a living interest in the subject, and with the understanding of one who had been already four times on the continent. I knew what had been accomplished by African explorers, and I knew how much of the dark interior was still unknown to the world.[15]

The interior of sexualized, racialized space became literal in Stanley's contemporary, James Marion Sims. The "father" of modern gynecology in North America, Sims experimented on the bodies of enslaved women in order to develop his signature procedure.[16] Gynecology at large in this era was "being formalized and legitimated on the reproductive organs and bodies of black women," Dierdre Cooper Owens writes in *Medical Bondage*.[17] Indeed as Cooper Owens' book demonstrates, gynecology was in part founded in this period to increase the capacities of enslaved women by "fixing" the injuries to their bodies incurred by rape and forced reproduction.

Race was not just the pretext of these gynecologists' medical knowledge, it was also the beating heart of their medical ruminations.[18] Nineteenth-century race science was diagnosing, and that is to say manufacturing, features as physiologically racial. Pelvimetry, for instance, which measured the size of a woman's pelvis to assess her ability to give birth, was a "racialized metalanguage" built on the house of cards of racial presumption, that was then trotted out to prove racial difference.[19]

But the inside of the body, its *interior*, was tricky. Gynecological medicine, Cooper Owens writes, "was one of the foremost fields in which the failures of race science were revealed.... Once doctors examined, excised, and sometimes preserved black women's sexual organs in jars, how could they accurately detect whether a burst ovary or a small cervix belonged to a black woman or a white woman?"[20] The ambiguities of social life were worked out through anatomical description.

In his narration of discovery of his signature procedure, Sims coolly describes the brutal details of his scenes of treatment, the prone positions of his subjects, the extremity of their pain—the room of doctors watching the violation. Their subjective interior flattened in the name of physical depth. While hailing his own prowess, he makes clear this was not work he enjoyed: "If there was anything I hated, it was investigating the organs of the female pelvis."[21]

These descriptions occur in his autobiography, *The Story of My Life*. Sims, it turns out, is a reluctant autobiographer: "Doctors seldom write autobiographies. They never have leisure, and their lives are not so full of adventure or incident as to be interesting to the general reader."[22] It was friends who suggested it. First, an old friend who had heard of his professional success, to which Sims responds with astonishment: "I was very much surprised, and blushed like a woman."[23] The second friend, a bedridden woman, pressed Sims for details about the more intimate dimensions of his life. At first he demurred. After all, for Sims—the celebrated inventor of the speculum—the interior was an ambivalent place. But she convinced Sims that he should not only account for his professional successes. He should also account, he concluded, for the "personal life"—for, in other words, the "inner man."[24]

## Interior: Garden

For the fourth-century theologian Gregory of Nyssa, virginity—and what he meant by "virginity" was ascetic sexual restraint—was a reflection of God's own purity.[25] Imagine water, he wrote, its smoothness, and the way it reflects the sun in slices. Imagine a mirror. Imagine now, he wrote, the mirror fogged with the louring vapor of desire. Imagine the dimming light. Imagine that virginity is an entryway, he said, a door to the brimming garden. Seasonless. Sweet, but not cloying. Somehow. Imagine entering. Imagine the door shuts.

Ambrose, the fourth-century bishop of Milan, writing on women's virginity, likewise thought of the garden and its door. But for him their *bodies* were the garden. He quotes the Song of Songs: "A garden enclosed is my sister, my spouse; a spring shut up, a fountain sealed."[26]

Openness and closure were what marked a body as female. There was, for instance, Hesiod's Pandora, the imagined first woman, and her metonymic jar, whose opening unleashed plagues.[27] But metaphor often became materiality, and the youth and then sexlessness of "virginity" gave way to a more common imagination of physical *intactness*.[28] Mary of Nazareth, the mother of Jesus, had more than a sexless conception. To writers in late antiquity, her body was unfazed even by giving birth. The mechanics needed untangling. They wrote, furiously, on whether and to what extent Mary could be said to be open or closed, and how.[29]

Ambrose was among them. Mary, forever enclosed, was a model, a mirror, he writes, for the life of other virgins.[30] Her physical enclosure, her sex contained, was also a model of silence for other virgins: the closing of the speaking mouth.[31] The bolted door.

Ambrose dreamed of confinement. But Ambrose, in speaking of the walled and sealed garden, began to remember those whirring tenders and tenants of the garden: bees.[32] Virginity was work, he cautioned, as his mind wandered toward that minor and studious labor. He thought of the gold hexagons of the honeycomb, the slow liquid of the tissued cells. He imagined, somewhere in the garden, the mandibles and tongues, the small turnings of pollen, of wax. This, he said, is the modest but sublime work of virginity, and nothing less. Nothing less than the work of mouths. The work of eating flowers.

## Interior: Fire

The third century *Protogospel of James* tells the story of Mary the mother of Jesus, from her own conception to the birth of Jesus. Mary herself was an unlikely birth to an infertile mother. A child whose purity (ritual, sexual) was guarded carefully, diligently, first by her parents, then, as time went on, by the priests of the temple to which she was dedicated. Always given over. So achingly unspoiled that she was hardly human. Something smaller, lighter: more bird than human. Fed lightly, out of the hands of angels. Touched, in fact, only by angels. Angels bringing her not just food but, eventually, the immeasurable gravity of pregnancy, the raw singe of labor. And then a baby, alien, the way babies are always alien. The midwife, suddenly yelling, "A virgin has given birth!"

"Show yourself."

The body as proof.

But when, in disbelief, Salome reached toward her, when her long flat hand tried to find something in Mary that it couldn't find, her fingers began to burn. Her hand breaking out like laughter. She gripped her wrist, as if to hold it off. It could not be held off.

[What I feared about giving birth was not the pain or the child. It was a fear of what else would come out of me. If given the chance to speak, what would my body say that it couldn't take back?]

"If black people are the subconscious of the Western mind, where is 'the black subconscious,' both individually and collectively articulated?" writes poet Elizabeth Alexander, in a reiteration of and response to Ntozake Shange.[33] Alexander continues: "My interest is not in psychotherapeutic culture and African American literature—though what a fascinating topic it is," Alexander continues, "but rather the marker such language offers for identifying complex and often unexplored interiority beyond the face of the social self."[34] Alexander describes her interest in black interiority and imagination not as a desire to find a part of the self untouched by the confinements of racialization, but rather as a desire to do justice to the ways black people imagine themselves and imagine living beyond those confinements. Black interiority is, among other things, a space of privacy and depth that exists on the other side of the presentational and representational demands of the white imagination. In some cases, Alexander says, black interiority is manifested in arrangements and embellishments of physical, private, or semi-private space: living rooms, for instance, or gardens.

In Kevin Quashie's reading of Alexander's essay, he notes the conundrums of trying to describe this interior: "Furthermore, the interior is mostly known through language or behavior, through exterior manifestations, and is therefore hard to know on its own terms.... And yet the interior is expressive; it is articulate and meaningful and has a social impact."[35] Quashie's book *The Sovereignty of Quiet* is a collection of portraits of black expressiveness other than the most visible, frequently recognized and visualized forms—namely, public resistance. Without doubting the historical and political importance of forms of black public resistance, Quashie points out through these various literary and visual portraits of black quietness just how much is missed when resistance, a direct response to white racism, is the only reading. Some of what is missed: moments of ambivalence, softness, and beauty. "In its magnificence, quiet is an invitation to consider black cultural identity from somewhere other than the conceptual places that we have come to accept as definitive of and singular to black culture," he writes, "not the 'hip personality' exposed to and performed to the world, but the interior aliveness, the reservoir of human complexity that is deep inside."[36] Quiet is, for Quashie, about depth and dignity, the nuance and possibility of the interior. Quiet is interiority's subtle, unresolved force and power. It is a potency that speaks under and past the flat façade of racialized subjectivity, a sort of speaking with and to oneself—wildly, wordless.

Interlude

## The Phoenix

> The new is an imperial incentive, a requirement, and a command....
> —ARIELLA AÏSHA AZOULAY, *Potential History*

No one wants to live into eternity,
no matter how deep the grove,
how sweet the shade. Even the saffron
sky at morning will stop filling you up,
as you haul yourself to the fountain
to sing, again,
some variation of the same tune.

Every day is a thousand years,
a thousand years in a day,
until finally you get your rest,
but then the rest turns
out to be fire,
turns out to be a great
conflagration of terrible hope,
taking you with it,
the cinders of you
another thing to
gather up, to fashion—
first into a milky worm,
next, a translucent egg.
You crack yourself open,
and before you know it
you're back at it—
the singing, the fountain
the whole procedure. Still,
each time, the mortals come
to watch you burn,
themselves dying
to become some novel thing.[1]

PART III

¤ \ ¤ / ¤

# Saints' Lives

## The Emperor Constantine's Death

We cannot compare him with that bird of Egypt,
        The bodies of great men are always smaller

the only one of its kind (they say) which dies
        than you think, splayed and suddenly paltry

self-sacrificed, in the sweet vapor and rising from its own ashes,
        the green gown open at the bottom, a furred creature,

newly alive, spiraling upwards its body unspoiled.
        breathing through the bellows of a machine.

Instead, he resembled his Savior who like planted corn
        Remember that speech he gave, hands gripping the pew,

proliferates from even a single grain, cropping up everywhere,
        steadying himself, already stiff and shaking?

the world a field for his gleaning. In every province, his statue
        Disease was only a fizz in his brain, still an idea,

appeared, great spire, stabbing the sky; that golden presence
        but gaining fast. We fed him with our gaze.

wresting from each of us the speaking of his name,
        We colluded in hardening him until he became effigy

forever, in astonished whispers.
        shocked and skeletal, alone, beloved reliquary.[1]

\*

"Let us begin with the sadness of late-Roman cemeteries. They were very large and full of very ordinary people."[2]

\*

"The phrase *slow death* refers to the physical wearing out of a population in a way that points to its deterioration as a defining condition of its experience and historical existence...."[3]

[Most of the time, I just wanted desperately to be alone.]

## Simeon on the Pillar

### 1

Don't tell me you have never tried to contrive your own escape, to fabricate it, to build it out of wood and nails, fiberglass, canvas, bits of iron, twine and glue, whatever you have. Mine was stone.

### 2

Although it ended with sky, it started with dirt. The prostrations began as digging. Legs cramping. Hair smelling of peat. I was buried chest high in the garden when they fished me out screaming.

### 3

It was never about being good. It was that silence like a locked house refused me. The touch of others broke me. It was the coarse and unbearable voice drawing me higher, but only literally, like Babel never happened. Like humility isn't always staged. There is no door between two realms here. Only the lead-white plaster floor. Only the chafing heartbeat of exhaustion as you pause, in the middle of your thousandth bow, arrested on a column of your own making.

## Antony Speaks After Solitude

Leave this world.

Leave its disappointments. Its slick patrons, whatever of yours that they want. The lure of minor power, its many tiny deaths. Leave the strung-out solace of speech, the straining for vindication.

I know who you are. You have nothing to lose but your spinelessness. Come to the desert and come alone. You must make your appearance before the one whose gaze dismantles, who calls to account in the name of love.

## Saint's Lives: Extremity

Precarity was, for them, the environment. The quality of the air. An incessant ringing in the ears. A pain beginning like a needle behind the eye. It was the environment of an empire trying to will itself into perpetuity.

Death and peril were the pulse of daily life in antiquity. Poverty and disease outbreaks (such as cholera) were part of the landscape, and easily fatal. There were the ordinary abuses at the hands of tax collectors, or Romans (soldiers and citizens) who appropriated the property of or otherwise violently dominated others.[4] Labor, enslavement, and migration, too, killed.[5] There was also the regular, constant deaths of children and women in childbirth, which contributed to an average lifespan of about twenty years.

In late antiquity, these conditions intensified. Geographical boundaries shifted. Constituencies changed. Wars raged almost continuously in the late third and early fourth centuries, but invasions from outsiders and civils wars were constants in late antiquity.[6] Two massive plagues, in the third and the sixth to eighth centuries, devastated the population.[7] "Late antiquity is a very rewarding period for the study of subsistence crises and epidemics," Dionysios Stathakopoulos writes. "During these five centuries the early Byzantine Empire reached its widest expansion and highest population density only to experience a sharp decline in both of them."[8] These constant deaths in particular meant an equally constant and forceful compulsion to guarantee the ongoing life of the family; the remaking of a population.[9] For every woman who died, another woman was needed.

It was a protracted state of "crisis ordinariness," such that it felt less like crisis, more like ordinariness.[10] The ringing got louder, higher in pitch.

Over this same long arc, there began another kind of intensification: an intensification of *restraint*. What belonged mostly to Stoic philosophy—abstention from sex and marriage, a disapproval of excess eating and drinking, the struggle to overcome strong feelings—began to pique others.[11] It gained momentum. An art of restriction, in the name of Christ. For some, it became extreme. The sublime fog of starvation. The enthralling distraction of a civil war with desire. It became as extreme as the landscape; as desperate and provisional.

## The Demons Address Antony

It's perpetual winter in this desert. You arrived fresh off your parents' death, leaving your sister. You turned to her and shrugged as you exited. Orpheus minus regret. Distance summoned you.

But we were always here. Poor tourist of privacy, what did you expect? We watched when the hunger finally got to you, watched the vowels forming, flimsy o's, in rings above your head. We watched your eyes and mouth dry out, your lips crack.

*Relief is possible*, we murmured, but the softer our voices got, the harder you bled. Surely you know that what lacerates you, what holds you down is not sex, or the trap of money, but the memory of your father's hands, your sister's need, barefaced and heavy as glass.

## Saint's Lives: Endurance

What then am I saying and writing? Nothing, Olympias, is equal to patience amidst upsetting circumstances for an account of good credit. For it is the queen of the goods and the very best garland of crowns.... —JOHN CHRYSOSTOM, *Letter to Olympias*, trans. Edward Vodoklys

The fourth-century Christian preacher with the golden mouth, John Chrysostom, writes to Olympias, a wealthy fellow ascetic, dear to him, while she is sick. She is in part sick with grief over his exile and their separation; she has been depriving herself to punish herself for this grief.[12] John too is sick, and describes the severity of his suffering by comparing his own trials to Job: not even the loss of his own children could drive Job to wish for death; it was *disease* that had him begging.[13] Sickness outdoes even John's exile in the difficulties it causes him.[14] For Olympias, too, her illness is worse (according to John) than literal torture, because she lives constantly with a metaphorical executioner.[15] But they should be consoled, he writes, by the fact that it is also a condition the endurance of which most guarantees salvation.

The saints were the truest models of endurance, and whose suffering could be brought in at any moment to offer examples and metaphors for less exceptional experiences. John's homilies indeed remind his audiences not just of the extraordinariness of the saints, but of his listeners' identification with the holy dead. Especially what they could endure. To be both humbled and inspired by their stamina.[16] To be, with the saints, unfazed by what bad fate the world had prepared for them. *To wait*. This was not about gratitude for getting away with less pain: a life full of hardship was a sign of being close to God.[17] It was about increasing one's capacity to bear a difficult world.

Ascetics and martyrs were known especially for their lengthy tortures, cosmic and statutory. There was, for instance, Saint Lucian, whose extended death by starvation was enacted by demons, ones who then tempt him with food sacrificed to foreign gods. Chrysostom imagines the scene vividly: "And, even though starvation was shouting loudly at him from within and urging him to touch what was lying in front of him, the fear of God stayed his hands and made him forget nature itself." Lucian, Chrysostom says, survived by conjuring another table, one "filled with the Spirit."[18]

Other saints were said to even plead to extend their own deaths. Palladius of Aspuna tells the story of Potamiaine, an enslaved girl who, after refusing to agree to be raped by her enslaver, is brought before the governor for judgment. He boils a cauldron of tar and gives her the choice to die in it or submit. So Potamiaine requests that she be lowered into the vat slowly, bit by bit, in a protest that also proves her forbearance.[19]

The saints were models of extremity. They were the ones who could survive with the least. Who lived the longest in the desert. Who performed the most austere acts. They were the ones who were the most lewd or promiscuous only to become the most pure-hearted. They were the wealthiest who gave the most up. Why? Because flourishing, they knew, was not of this world. "Don't, please," the man with the golden mouth pleads, "don't let's plan so badly for ourselves and for our salvation, but look to these saints, these noble and brave athletes, who have been given to us in place of torches, and amend our own life to their courage and patience, so that after we depart this life by their prayers we might be able to both see and embrace them and be assigned to their heavenly dwellings."[20] They were all to bear it, like the Israelites in exile, forty years in the desert, before getting anything like respite. The blessings were always yet to come.

Ascetic practitioners were learning to tolerate, like Potamiaine, increasingly perilous conditions. To imagine those conditions not as peril or privation, but as accomplishment and transformation. Each fast, each illness, and each long, arduous day a way of increasing the threshold for pain, an attenuation to an environment of escalating vulnerability. Both muting and amplifying the effects of that environment—as Olympias's illness shows, self-control can easily tip back over into vulnerability. And the tension with the world was only on the surface, for in their aspiration to extend the threshold, physical or emotional, in the name of salvation, they were also quietly rationalizing and sustaining the ongoing catastrophe that *was* their world. A world that demanded they always *bear more*, or at the very least, simply *go on*.

Endurance is suffering plus time. John's deliberate storytelling style also played out his preoccupation with endurance, with waiting, with the meaningful descriptive pause.[21] He practices this in his own retelling of the story of Noah and the flood in Genesis, in which John himself, like and with Noah, stays suspended for an extended length of time afloat in the abyss: "For a whole year, he lived in this strange and novel prison, unable even to breath fresh air—for how could he, when the ark was closed in on all sides? Tell me: how did he put up with it? How did he endure it?"[22] Snagged for a moment, caught in his own pause, the man with the golden mouth imagined the waves crashing on the sides of the boat, the uncertainty, the rising water. He imagined the water's depths, its violence. He imagined its endless horizon.

[Not knowing what else to do, we worked at all hours.]

## Macrina Teaches a Course on Grief

So I went to her, wanting to share the loss of our brother. My soul was sorrow-stricken by this grievous blow, and I wanted someone who could feel it equally, to mingle my tears with. But when we were in each other's presence, the sight of her, my teacher, awakened all of my pain. She was lying in a state close to death. She gave in to me for a little while, like a skilled driver in the ungovernable violence of my grief, and then tried to keep me in check with her words, to correct the indiscipline of my soul.... "Only men without hope have these feelings." —GREGORY OF NYSSA, *On the Soul and Resurrection*[23]

Macrina teaches a course on grief. Gregory takes notes. His notes say: feel nothing. His notes say: body = visible, soul = invisible. Body = moon, soul = sun? Ask later. Macrina quotes scripture, Plath, and Lear. A history of grief. Grief and subjectivity. She speaks effortlessly under the bad fluorescents, her voice echoing down the long hallway as if speaking through the vents. Grief versus melancholy. Grief and nationalism. The bibliography is extensive. Gregory plays devil's advocate, raises his hand, and asks about death. About wanting to live. About buckling at the knees at the glint of rain, starving alive for whatever god swept his arm to bring it. About how to love and not feel wrecked at loss. Macrina delivers a mini-lecture on hope. I too have lost, she says brightly, tightly. She pities him, sees a boy who has much to learn. Passion saves no one. She writes it on the board. At the bar the students call her Patron Saint of Robots and Machines. She knows this. Later Macrina sits Gregory down in her office in the University of Grief, her voice grey with transcendence, and tells him how she cured her own tumored heart with one little needle. Believe me, he says, I have seen the scar. I will forever be your student.

## Saint's Lives: Family

When the bridegroom looks upon the face of his beloved, the fear of separation immediately comes over him; while he listens to her sweet voice, he is aware that sometime he will not hear it... Assume that the moment of childbirth is at hand; it is not the birth of the child, but the presence of death that is thought of, and the death of the mother anticipated. —GREGORY OF NYSSA, *On Virginity*

"But in genealogical terms the bodies of human owners act simply as extensions of the matter and life of the house. The presumption in the text is that the human actors will disappear before the property does...." Catherine Michael Chin, "Apostles and Aristocrats"

Stories of the saints are often framed by the deaths of family members: Antony's parents, Melania the Younger's children, Gregory and Macrina's brothers. In other cases, or at the same time, they are marked by the abandonment of family: its responsibilities, its blanket compulsions to continuity.[24] Its demands to carry on, to shoulder the structure. Its demand to support a legacy you did not choose, one to which your own life was only incidental. Family and home, then, were often bad souvenirs of unethereal futures, guarantors of loss.

Jerome, writing to Eustochium after her mother Paula's death, describes Paula leaving her mundane life for the spiritual promise of the desert. He draws out one scene in particular—the scene of Paula's departure. Her children beg her to stay. What mother could leave? any reader (or Eustochium) might think. Or rather, what *kind* of mother? Paula was very torn, he emphasizes (perhaps to let her off the hook), as the separation of parent and child is one of the worst hardships one can sustain. Still, he notes, her eyes were dry as her love of God overcame her love of her children.[25]

But in an earlier letter, one to Paula herself, Paula is not as unshakeable as she was—or perhaps as Jerome posthumously imagined her to be—when she first set off. Jerome has to console Paula on the loss of her daughter, Blesilla, who dies as a result of her severe ascetic program. Who could blame a parent, he writes, for crying over the loss of their child? Yet, he says, when he thinks of the ascetic and the Christian, the mother disappears from view.[26] Commitment to Christ absents the mother, either in body or mind: she and her cares vaporize like fine mist. Jerome reminds Paula of Melania the Elder's steely example, her grief over deaths in her own family denied or deferred: "She didn't cry at all," he writes. "She stood there, motionless, and casting herself at Christ's feet, she smiled, as if she held him in her hands. She said,

'I am ready to serve you, Lord, for you have freed me from this burden.'"[27] Was the burden she was spared her grief or her family?

Indeed in Jerome's phantom chain of tearless mothers, it is hard to say which was more agonizing, more sad: the having of family, or the losing of it. Or rather the tearless mothers in Jerome offer an impossible pedagogy on how not to lose, each mother sailing off on a sea of tears they did not or could not cry. For Gregory of Nyssa, the solution was simple: the less family you had, the less you had to lose. But in all cases they seem to say that family, with all its promises and pressures, its attachments and terrible gravity, is always the very first scene of losing. It is where we first learn to lose.

### The Life of Saint Melania the Younger

Using as her reason the death of her child, she then put away all her silk dresses.

Although because of the delicacy of their youth, they then were not able to devote themselves entirely to intense asceticism, but they at least wore cheap clothes. —*The Life of Saint Melania the Younger*, trans. Papaloizos and Clark

> Even the language she spoke was textiles,
> cashmere, brocade, cervelt, vicuña,
> and that's how she knew she had to get out,
> to become a woman of some substance—
> of what substance? A different substance, earthier—
> muslin, cotton, linen. It took time, her skin chafed
> from the low thread counts, a rash
> like sleeping in cold grass, she was sans moisturizer,
> and while she waited to become substantial, while she
> waited for Spirit to be pulled from her
> like a single gauzy thread, she wondered
> (the haute couture now in plastic)
> if there was something more decadent
> than luxury clothes. She came up with praise,
> found it, quaint, like an old clip-on earring,
> the answer to what would feed her desire for opulence.
> Her children dead, what was left
> but the love of others, or at least the aura,
> draped over her like its own gossamer fabric?
> And so the story of all she had
> became a story of all she had given up.
> Praise her, praise her, praise her,
> the rich invent their own genres.

## Melania the Younger to Her Grandmother

Dying, you handed me the keys, and with them
a hundred empty rooms. *Have these*, you said
the words decomposing in your mouth.

I prayed you would teach me restraint—
lit candles on my dresser, taped pictures of you
over my bed. It was the altar, I was the votive,
counterfeit and still. Long before you died,
you left me that most grim bequest:
your name.[28]

## Perpetua, Martyr and Mother

First Perpetua was tossed around, and she fell on her groin. And when she sat up she pulled down the tunic, torn on the side, to conceal her thigh, mindful of modesty instead of pain. Then, having asked for a hairpin, she pinned up her hair which had been mussed. For it was not fitting for a martyr to suffer with disheveled hair.... —*The Martyrdom of Perpetua and Felicity*, trans. Cobb and Jacobs

We could not leave the house without her hair done, and dressing rooms were hard. Her restless covering of her own softness, no matter how slight. There was her stomach or arms, always something she tugged the cotton sweater over. Each bathing suit a trial from which my sister and I learned the delicate aesthetics of avoiding shame.

    I however craved her body, one longer than I would ever be, freckled in only the most beautiful places, almost ethereal sliding on skirts, me behind her with my dark fluffed hair in the many-mirrored room. She did not like my head in her lap, or my sister playing with her hair, and I imagine the theater in her mind where she was armed with a modesty she did not choose, where no pleasure or pain could undo her impulse to keep everything in place. I think about her leaving my father to go do what she had to do, which was live bravely without anyone; about how satisfyingly true it is that she was a victim, just not a victim of him. And I have never asked, but wonder how much of my childhood, until she could leave, she spent wanting to die.

## The Work of Grief

Rather, I am probing what kinds of slow deaths have been ongoing that a suicide might represent an escape from. —JASBIR PUAR, *The Right to Maim*

I could not anticipate how much of my work would be grieving for my students. What I thought would be aberrations or interruptions—their breakdowns over pressures to perform, their financial exigencies, the violences done to them, their deaths—turned out to be much of the landscape of teaching itself. This was especially true over a period in which a spate of suicides, including students I had taught, punctured the presumptions on which our tiny and insular campus operated. I lived in a house at the bottom of campus, 300 feet from one of the dorms. Cold dread rising every time a siren sounded; I checked my email for another note from the college president expressing shock and grief.

Shock and grief. Suicide has long been one of the top two causes of death on college campuses, and the rate of suicides among teens and young adults continues to climb.[29] It is no coincidence that when postsecondary education is billed as a guarantor of class status or financial stability, college becomes a place where many students register for the first time, if implicitly, the irreconcilability of American aspirations and American realities.

Jasbir Puar's *The Right to Maim* is a book about the liberal state mechanisms that offer the promise of inclusion for some disabled subjects, while at the same time perpetually creating populations that are wearied, worn, debilitated in various ways. The book begins with a section entitled "The Cost of Getting Better."[30] It hinges on a critique of Dan Savage's viral "It Gets Better" campaign, a campaign that hopes to wrench queer, depressed teens back from the risks of suicide. These risks are imagined primarily as a product of bullying. As Puar notes, though, Savage's campaign made a number of promises it couldn't keep: eventual security, safety, and upward mobility.[31] In other words: It promised access to a certain normativized picture of queer flourishing, one that presumes a white, cis, middle-class subject. Puar points to how Savage's campaign, while wanting to keep queer teens on the side of life, does so by implicitly imagining a life "after" queer trauma (a hard enough case to make), and by corralling them toward nationalist-capitalist economic projects. How, then, she wonders, do we think about those debilitated subjects who are unable or unwilling to join this project? What about the implicit aligning of health and normativity in the very notion of "getting better"? Is queer life, or any life, only meaningful, livable, if it can be recuperated toward this kind of future? "From this vantage, [It Gets Better] reflects a desire for the reinstatement of (white) racial privilege that was lost by being gay, one that is achievable through equality rights agendas like gay marriage and participation in neoliberal consumer culture."[32]

"It Gets Better" imagines and generates a collective in waiting: waiting for a future that it becomes more difficult with each passing day to see. Outside of the specificity of queer adolescent experiences, we could consider the relationship between horizons of promise, their nebulousness or collapse, and suicide. The relentless striving of college students toward ever more ephemeral goals, a realization that graduation is not an end to that striving but only a marker within its endlessness, is perhaps not incidental to the steep rate of suicide on college campuses.

We have yet to fully appreciate the ways college can be a space of spiritual death. But what else would one expect from institutions with their insatiable desires for financial growth, their bureaucracies, their evaluative and transactional framing of human relations, their structural exploitations? Out of these mundanities emerges a crisp pedagogy of the value of lives and living. And that spiritual death is in few places more obvious than in the collective institutional responses to student suicides. Think for instance of the administrative emails after the suicides: shock and grief, more shock, more grief. Will the grief ever end? What is the worth, to put it bluntly, of this administrative shock? Classes cancelled for one day after the first suicide. But after the others, simply "counseling is available" (for ten sessions only), and loudly proclaimed commitments to "wellbeing." After a suicide, grief might (*might*) create a pause—in classes, in talking about subject matter—but the pause is brief, and grief quickly morphs from interruption to part of the work: the care-taking work of the faculty and staff, for instance, or the institutional spin about teaching students to "fail forward" and not be crushed by disappointment. Resilience as limitless fortitude to endure.[33]

The labor of grief, of reassurance, of producing resilience, is arduous, and it inevitably redounds to the institution, the horizon of which is always uninterrupted flow: of capital, of evaluation and credentialing. It should be no surprise then that residents of the institution more than occasionally occur to themselves as captives of this flow, trapped in its relentless demand for strength and patience in an eternal futurity, and find themselves staring into the face of the deep.

## Mary of Egypt

### 1

When they find you naked in the desert, they only see their own pleasure. When you say, God did this to me, they only see redemption.

### 2

What if, before this, I was happy? The boat's lilt. My face, full and private as the water. When we arrived on shore, I went into the church for warmth.

### 3

The desert is ocean without depth. Vastness without motion. At night, I fantasize about drowning in sky.

### 4

I watch birds all day in this heat. Have you seen the way desert ravens lean forward to yell out? That's how I was back then. I used to speak into the world with my whole body.

## Saints' Lives: Choice

In Potamiaine's story, she must decide to either submit to being raped or enter the vat of tar. A drama of choice. Palladius's tale seems to offer the tantalizing possibility that even in the most dire straits, there are choices to be made, if stark ones. And for Palladius, Potamiaine chooses bravely and correctly. But the choice she is given, to be raped or die, is hardly one at all. In this landscape, the stakes of choice are enormous and the consequences inevitably bad.

In *Cruel Optimism*, Lauren Berlant diagnoses contemporary adaptations to the collapse of hopes for an American "good life" as the promise of this good life becomes ever more distant and ephemeral. In trying to better name the conditions of living in this state of gradually collapsed fantasy, Berlant foregrounds zones of existence "where life building and the attrition of human life are indistinguishable."[34] Where working toward your future is also diminishing it. This conceptual shift means reconfiguring the way we understand structural power and responses to it—including dramas of choice, which are imaginations of autonomy, and idealized mirror images of sovereign governmentality.[35]

Agency is something other than choice. It can be nonwillful interruption, or even, as Saba Mahmood famously argued, a kind of passivity that is also a technique of managing conditions without choosing, refusing, or vanquishing them.[36] Berlant theorizes what kind of agencies might be thinkable when sovereign governmentality is not the only or best way to describe life under power—especially structural violence that appears much more diffused into and across life. Berlant suggests, with Cressida Heyes following them, the very undramatic extension of regular activities (eating, drinking, drugs) as one such response, a kind of "lateral agency," in which grief for structural conditions lives, ambiently and undefined, in the body and psyche.[37] Notably, late capitalism is defined by a certain imagination of choice, and those choices are usually spectacularly inconsequential and consumerist, but fantasized to be part of one's own self-elaboration through consumer objects and brands: what to watch, eat, play, and so on. "Choice" in that context becomes both endless and elusive. What's more, so many of these choices end up contributing to the very ambivalent enactment of grief in the body, its impulse to numb and recline itself into minor relief, a kind of melancholic and oblique agency that only briefly interrupts the march of durational depletion.

Choice is a sharply drawn romance, a contrast to the faint and blurry lines of such lateral or passive agencies. The ultimate consequences for choices in stories of martyrs and saints only underline the eventfulness of choice. But are these romances of choice not the stories we love—the stories of extraordinary figures, whose adversity and resilience dwarf ours? Whose travails transform them, and for the better? In these stories, the infinite and daily minor decisions around how to live—the order in which to do errands, how to respond to children, whether or not you're up for sex—are vulcanized into one singular magnificent moment of choosing to, for example, leave for the desert, or, for martyrs, to revoke your loyalties or die.

In other ascetic literature, for example the *Rules* of Pachomius, the founder of roughly a dozen monasteries in upper Egypt, or the *Institutes* of John Cassian, the monk who translated Egyptian monastic life for the western part of the empire, we see just how much weight the decisions of the everyday could carry. They give instructions on the order of the day, precisely how monks should dress, how they should pray, how they should sleep, their disposition at meals, and what they should eat, how to manage desire, and why these things mattered as monks attempted to cultivate a particular and carefully titrated subjective state, to manage their capacity for discomfort, for doing without. Indeed, any small act (laughing at dinner) carried spiritual ramifications. And that is some of the work of this literature: in the unending maintenance of the monolithic mundane it endows each ordinary moment with the incandescence of the cosmic.

Who will spare us from full confrontation with the futility and tedious chaos of daily life? The examples and exhortations and encomiums of saints, with their cheerful labor, their triumphs over demons, and (of course) their otherworldly capacity for tolerance of intolerable conditions, are not just about a desire for virtue. Within the carrying on of the catastrophic quotidian, they are about a desire to master the scenes of one's own depletion. Even more, they are about a desire for consequence itself.

## Golden Girl (St. Aurea)

Somewhere in the sea is a stone once tied to the neck of a saint. The saint's name means "golden girl," in the same way any of us are, briefly, girls made of gold, briefly a statuette, blinding in beauty or power, raising children from the dead, immune to accusation, floating like a missile through the air, cutting it, unbreakable. I think of the stone, the weight of it, what it took to break her, corrode her, spine like a rod as they herded her into the boat. My grandmother once described my hair as the color of ripe wheat, beheld my glint. I was stitched into the cosmos then, every cell, and never since.

# Interlude

## On First Principles

And who is so silly to believe that God, after the manner of a farmer, "planted a paradise eastward in Eden," and set in it a visible and palpable "tree of life." ... I do not think anyone will doubt these are figurative expressions.... —ORIGEN, *On First Principles*

>What a fool, I too have craved a garden
>and was handed instead a metaphor. No calm cool.
>No ceanothus. An open valence at best.
>When I saw the ocean of ash, for instance, I asked for
>apricot trees, for azalea, and got the bottomless
>reservoir of meaning. So too I saw the bombed hospital.
>Idiot that I am, I wanted periwinkle. I got the perilous mirror.
>I saw children buried under buildings.
>I begged for marigold, hydrangea. Got the rotten intangible. God,
>it turns out, is no gardener. Every day extremity reinvents itself.
>The children accumulate in the ground.
>I asked for petal and stem, but got its petty simulation.
>I took its fast taste like cotton candy in your mouth on the last
>day of the fair. I wanted bridlewreath. I wanted soil. I wanted pine.

PART IV

¤ \ ¤ / ¤

# The Passing World

\*

"It is not whether, at some point between Marcus Aurelius and Constantine ... a watershed was passed. The real problem is what it is like for a great traditional society to pass over a watershed."[1]

[How to document a passing world?]

### The Last Oracle at Delphi (to the Emperor Julian)

Tell the emperor
there is no advice.

My hall has fallen
to the ground.

Apollo no longer has his house
nor his mantic laurel,
nor his prophetic spring.

The speaking water
has gone silent.[2]

### Libanius: A Monody on the Temple of Apollo, Destroyed by Fire

or, as it is said, by lightning. It was not lightning. No storms, only the rippling waft of gasoline, the air sharp as the arsonist's laughter. What lit first, the roof, your face, your crown? Jupiter, that coward, delivered no rain.

Deep in the groves, we also burned. Where will we hide ourselves? Who that came to you didn't find peace? What malady couldn't you cure? The deity once kissed by the emperor has vanished.

You who weakened the will of despots with your beauty: What traitor struck the match? And how did he not stop dead, lovesick for your unmarred skin, your open mouth, you so perpetually clean shaven and locked in song?[3]

## Dedications to the Old Gods: Zeus

You would appear at my porch like a storm, prefaced by stillness and the taste of metal. Your arrival a reminder that even my child was yours for the taking. A castoff of your largesse.

    With time, you only got smaller. You watched my obeisances hollow, the copper sun rise on a city glittering without you. Go ahead, bring me your rage. I'm drunk with cavalier sin. What can you do, archaic and sunken within the new order?

## Dedications to the Old Gods: Demeter

Fall comes early, and with it the memory of you and the spreading ink of your encroaching mood. The slouching at the table, tea cold; the long showers and wordless stares.

Who am I now, without your sorrow to house me? Without its relief, when you finally got out of bed and found the world, and us, worthy of your care? We were afflicted with you, your depletion but also your warmth, your sighing laughter a soft inauguration—we opened to you—when this, all this, was yours, a province of hapless seasons.

### Dedications to the Old Gods: Hades

I begged you to leave me alone but it was the begging that I loved. Portal gone, I laid down by the river, now narrowed to a vein, with a coin under my tongue. Hoping to be taken.

I tried to die to find you. But in this new world, you can only die into more light. What I wanted was the low-pitched relief of shadows. To get ferried, breathless, through your inscrutable kingdom. To be caught in the falling mist of your ambient threat.

### Dedications to the Old Gods: Aphrodite

You, sovereign presider over marriage, could draw me stumbling and crashing through my own house to you. Could ask me to shatter any delicate thing—a plate, a bone, a vow—and I would for the chance to stand before you and pray by pressing against your implacable chest. To crumple at your indifference. This is the only fidelity that matters.

Outside, they wait, ready to discredit you. Inside, from this stupor, you have lost nothing.

## The Last Pagan Emperor

The last pagan emperor, Julian, was born Christian in a Christian world, to possibly the most famously Christian family in history. His uncle Constantine, whose sudden and late-breaking devotion to Christ, arriving like a ghost in the night and during the ambiguities of war, formalized Christianity's status among the elite, and quickly multiplied the Christian clutter strewn across the empire. But what Julian saw when he saw the colossal and spectacular churches in Rome or Jerusalem was not splendor: he saw a passing world at risk of bastardization. He saw a world impoverished by its own novelty, divorced from the integrity of its past. The Christian god was an innovation, changeable, and irrational in his jealousy.[4] What's worse, Christian writers were derivative. They skimmed from the top of Greek culture, and bent Greek philosophy away from its source, away from the gods that enabled it.[5]

Julian's love of philosophy, by contrast, was ardent and true. His love of the gods a knowledge almost primordial in him—a spirit called to the wellspring. "For I am a follower of King Helios," Julian writes, "And of this fact I possess within me, known to myself alone, proofs more certain than I can give."[6] For a moment, Julian reminisces: "From my childhood an extraordinary longing for the rays of the god penetrated deep into my soul; and from my earliest years my mind was so completely swayed by the light that illumines the heavens that not only did I desire to gaze intently at the sun, but whenever I walked abroad in the night season, when the firmament was clear and cloudless, I abandoned all else without exception and gave myself up to the beauty of the heavens."[7] Julian warmed.

Helios: a god prior to all the others. The timeless, changeless god whose movement across the sky produces time and change.[8]

It was a difficult childhood. He was born in Christianity's capital, during his uncle's reign. Christian empire was his royal birthright. But at six he was without parents: his mother had died when he was a toddler, his father was murdered in Constantine's sons' attempt to grab power after the death of their father.[9] Much of Julian's childhood was spent in exile, where he read and learned voraciously with his tutor and caretaker, Mardonius. "It was only his passion for study ... that preserved his sanity...."[10] What he read were the Greek classics, which generated a world for him more real than the world itself.[11]

Julian drew up his love of philosophy and the traditional gods in the image and shadow of Christian thought—thought that was also formed in and through the Greek philosophical tradition.[12] He was one generation removed from a world ruled by Zeus and Apollo, born decades after Constantine's wartime vision of the cross, but only a year after a statue of Constantine depicted to imply Helios was erected in Constantinople.[13] That is, the philosophy and piety to which Julian devoted himself was always an epitomized one, a tangled remembrance of a pure past he never lived. Despite his excessive power and ambition, in other words, Julian's devotion was strikingly guileless. He craved a bygone time, one purer and more authentic than the time he knew, one as bright and fixed as the sun.

\*

"Insofar as the emperor's presence in the holy places was inscribed through the Roman monumentalization of the Christian past, it is fitting that one of Constantine's most important constructions in the holy city [of Jerusalem], the Church of the Holy Sepulchre, commemorates a sacred absence: the celestial body of the risen Jesus."[14]

[Something was always missing.]

## Sodom and Return

And when he concocted this plan to rebuild the Jerusalem temple, and made the Jews believe it... they began to argue about how it should be rebuilt. And in large numbers with great enthusiasm they started the work. Not only did women rip off their jewelry and offer it for the temple, they even carried away the dirt in the skirts of their dresses, sparing neither their precious clothes, nor the tenderness of their bodies.—GREGORY OF NAZIANZUS, *Oration 5*

After Julian's death, the late fourth-century Christian theologian Gregory of Nazianzus writes to seal Julian's reputation as "apostate," and conjures this scene: upon learning of Julian's plan to rebuild the temple, Jews—ones, by Gregory's account, too gullible to question Julian's seriousness or motive—fight and trip over themselves, cart dirt by the armful, practically electrified by the promise. But almost as soon as they begin the construction, Gregory says, the otherworldly intervenes: a wind blows the gates shut, an earthquake and a fire follow, causing injury, death, and disarray. God has embarrassed the Jews wanting to recover their site of worship if not also their sovereignty, and righted the cosmos, signing his intervention by stamping a cross in the sky with light. Gregory depicts the Jewish crowds running from the scene with a cruelly comic air: duped by the emperor—who wanted primarily to upset Christians—punished by God, and scrambling for cover, they are undone by their own hope and nostalgia.[15]

In his attempt to insult Julian, Gregory trots out a series of villains from the Hebrew Bible, likening Julian to Jeroboam, Ahab, the Pharoah, Nebuchadnezzar. But the entire scene is drawn up with reference to Hebrew scriptural stories, including the suggestion that those burnt up in the fire might be reminiscent of the destruction of Sodom in Genesis 19, and that those maimed in the chaos would be a "living monument" to not just their "sin," but God's catastrophic rage.[16]

In associating Jews with Sodomites, Gregory has made them outsiders in their own history, an especially bleak Christian rhetorical move. But to evoke Sodom is to evoke a story not just of a sinful city burned to the ground. It is to evoke a story of *looking back*: Lot and his wife, on their way safely out of Sodom with their family, are given the instruction to not turn and see the rain of sulfur and ash. Lot's wife cannot resist, and whether out of curiosity, defiance, or compassion (we can't say), she turns around and casts her glance backward. God, extending the violence to any connection to the city, turns her into a pillar of salt.

The implicit moral of Genesis 19 is to face forward, to let the old city burn. It is a message, one could imagine, Gregory would have directed at the Jews and Julian alike. The irony is that Gregory cannot send that message without making his own appeals to some of those same pasts. His vitriol against Julian and the Jews in his story might resonate then as fighting any attachment to the past that obstructs the promised arrival of a Christian future. It was an arrival that felt, at the time, neither grand nor glorious. Held in the suspense of that glittering near-future, Gregory and his contemporaries could, and did, rewrite the past as a Christian story.

But the past begs return and, frustratingly enough, the past has a life beyond writing. What's more, there's no predicting what you might see when you look there. Two decades after Gregory writes this oration, in a more securely Christian empire, the Christian tourist Egeria found herself, during her three-year pilgrimage, at the sacred site of this same biblical story, casting her own glance backward. In her journal, she walks her sisters at home through her visit: "To our left was the whole country of the Sodomites, including Zoar, the only one of the five cities which remain today."[17] She stands on that holy ground, but there is little to witness to either its history or its holiness: "There is still something left of it; but all that is left of the others is heaps of ruins, because they were burned to ashes."[18] In a text full of breathless descriptions of romanticized places and encounters, at this moment, she readies her sisterly readers for disappointment: Egeria cannot see even the most distinctive monument in that place, the pillar of salt. It is now covered by the sea, the physical source of Gregory's malicious comparison gone. And Egeria, like the woman-made-monument she seeks—the one turned to gunmetal white grit from her feet to her craned neck to her open, wet eyes—is left witnessing only to its passing.

[There was no going back, even as it seemed there was no moving forward. This conundrum followed them wherever they went.]

### Postcards from Egeria: Sinai

Writing to you from the mountain of God
where the children of Israel waited,
restless, for Moses to come down,
where they forgot what it was all for
and liquified their jewelry,
fashioning a beast. Writing
from where Moses returned, engulfed
by his own frustration,
burning that resplendent metal animal
and dumping the blond ashes
in the water, writing from where the people
drank their own gold, the misdeed
irradiating their bodies.
I will bring back a sloshing jar of the water.
I saw the bush and it did not burn.

## Postcards from Egeria: Jerusalem

I don't know why I left,
only that I needed to be elsewhere,
unable to stay in the lurid
period drama of the present,
its unmoral story.

I longed to inhale the musky perfume of meaning.
I saw the cross of Jesus.
Very warm days with lots of walking.

## Postcards from Egeria: Seeing the Saints

I came all this way to see saints—
walked toward extremity,
hoping to stare into the burnt
stars of their eyes,
hoping to see for myself
their hallowed skeletal limbs,
to see the unequivocal proof
that God speaks,
and speaks through pain.

Instead I found myself
in the desert no one tells you about:
among almond trees, the pink
flowering tamarisk,
and acacia like gawky parasols.
In the rain,
things greened.

It was alive, bereft of demons.
Its mildness an offense.
I was desolate.
I wanted desolation.

[It was a world they did not recognize, even as it was a world of their making.]

Eusebius with his feet in the sand, under a pocked and amber moon, wondering at the water's depths: *What lived in there, what died?* How would he ever know?

[They had learned only one way to hope. That, too, was passing.]

## The City of God, Taking Its Sweet Time

But the actual possession of the happiness of this life, without the hope of what is beyond, is a false happiness, and a profound misery. —AUGUSTINE, *City of God*

It will not last. You probably know that already,
with this unseasonably cold Spring, the forsythia slouching,
weighed down with the faint brutality of an April snow.
But its ending goes on forever, constantly heralded,
each day new evidence, a new threshold passed.
Your nerves fray with the waiting, you try your
exercises of gratitude, reminding yourself
of what you'll miss, getting nostalgic in advance
for the rotting oak, for the paint-peeled windows
and all the things that come through them—light breezes,
bird sounds, whatever—the next city will have better
things, but it will not have these things, so you wake up
extra early to sit on the porch and watch the horizon ease
from dark to dim, take in this view, a view you will not
have in the next city, put on Schubert or Chopin, something
a little schmaltzy, so you can pretend you're not at arm's
length from all of these good things, pretend you're not losing
your mind because you are, after all, still here; this city, this life is still
here, always and forever in the middle of closing.

### Prudentius, Hymn for December 25th

Why are the days so narrow, the sun a single, thinning bar?
Did Christ not warm the skies, widening that slab of light?

Winter slants towards us, increasingly sharp. Let the air mellow again,
let the earth waste itself with color. Christ, this is the day

on which the Father coughed you into the world and covered you
in mud: your body a bulb for a raging Spring. You sobbed at the entry.

Appear, sweet boy, double agent. The Father marshaled us with your
  birth.
He could not let us be stolen, left to smoke. Not his arresting planet,
  endlessly baroque.

Child, did you not end this white age, its languor and violence?
Why this sky, this cold ether, of iron and silence?

# Epilogue

## Metamorphoses

It was a time of change. In this, it was like all times. Dull on the face of it. You lean over the sink, spit, switch the laundry. You tire of meal prep, find comfort in the single file line of commuters blinking onto the highway, feel something bright and essential draining even from daybreak.

You listen to the neighbors argue on the sidewalk in the early hours, they haven't had breakfast yet, just met the sunrise spent and pleading. They don't know that part of change is going unrecognized at home. That we are not dynasts of change, at best its jacks and jokers. The man wishing to become a bird becomes an ass. Children start to talk back. We were promised something else, we say, our mouths full of roses.

They don't know that what they're fighting is an atmosphere gathering around them. That everywhere craters are opening in the ground, that the radio is increasingly static.

Maybe they know. Maybe they sense the atmosphere gathering, and find the plodding choreography of traffic lights, stop, go, pause, to be a portent of the sacrosanct, garish but real. They petition each other for their lives, the soft electricity of the air breathing through them, their city of smashed glass only the in-breaking of a world to come.

# Appendix

The second century CE to the sixth century CE in Christian history is a period often painted as a movement from victimhood (persecution and martyrdom in the second and third centuries) to imperial religion (with Constantine, the first Christian emperor, in the fourth century). Much scholarship has complicated the simplicity of that arc, suggesting that while it is true that the status and number of Christians changed remarkably over this time, Christian martyr stories were not exactly reflective of actual events, and the Roman empire "becoming Christian" was no straightforward or unilateral affair. These are positions I also hold; this book takes these positions for granted.

### Notes for Part I (Fathers)

### "Fathers"

The study of late ancient Christianity emerged in part from "Patristics," called such for its foundational emphasis on "the church fathers"—generally elite and influential figures like Origen, Athanasius, Jerome, Augustine—whose names are associated with great volumes of texts. These men were academics. Although the term "Patristics" has faded, the field's reliance on these figures as *authors* and even its veneration of these figures as historical personalities survives.[1] "Fathers" here is shorthand then for the kinds of authority accrued in and through texts, writing, intellectual work—whether that authority is enacted, desired, or projected. In co-voicing with some of these figures, I hope to interrupt these author-effects, including their authority.

### Chronography

The second century *Chronography* attributed to Julius Africanus was an attempt to tell a history of the world from the biblical creation, one "substantiated" with the timelines of the histories of other peoples, such as the Egyptians and the Phoenicians. Ironic to its aspirations toward comprehensiveness, *Chronography* comes to us now only in fragments. This poem also plays with another work attributed to Africanus, called *Embroideries*, an encyclopedic synthesis of bodies of knowledge that ranges across interests in natural history, agriculture, the military, and pharmacology.

### Eusebius of Caesarea

The *Chronography* was an influence on the Christian bishop Eusebius of Caesarea's own time-management projects, *Church History* and *Chronicle*, begun in the late third century. The *Chronicle* combined the historical traditions of different cultures into a tabular system. Eusebius attempted to synchronize biblical history with Greek and Roman history, producing a comprehensive "world history" invested especially in illustrating the universal centrality and importance of Jewish and Christian events. *Church History* is similarly interested in chronology, periodization, and is in part a history of salvation. Overall, Eusebius's texts, as Scott Johnson has argued, cast time as a "succession of moments."[2] More than that, they produce time as something to be mastered and transcended.

### Grammarians

1. Grammar in late antiquity was a practice of textual concentration, fragmentation, and isolation. I am fascinated by Michael Chin's work (cited as epigraph to the poem) which shows not only how class is produced in this linguistic practice of fragments. This practice also produced the idea of the classical past, mainly as something to uphold and preserve, even as it produced a sense of being Christian as a momentary temporal fragment.
2. The etymological root of *philology* is "love."

### Jerome

The figure that appears through Jerome's writings (late fourth/early fifth century) is an unappealing one, what with his heated interest in both language and women—converging most distinctly in his letters advising women on education, marriage, and bodily comportment.[3] Most famous now for his Latin translations of biblical texts, and his association with the "dynamic equivalence" theory of translation (see Epistle 57, to Pammachius), Jerome's writings, produced in an assertive age of Christian dominance, exploit Jewish texts and knowledge to produce Christian truth.[4]

### Apophasis

Apophatic theology is a style of writing popular in late antiquity that indexes a certain distrust in words for getting at the reality of God, even while using lots of verbal formulations, posed negatively, to do it. Writers feeling and denying the limits of their own work in language.

NOTES FOR PART II (*NOTES FROM THE INTERIOR*)

### Interiority

Scholars have argued about the origins of the [notion of the] interior self, sometimes locating those origins in late antiquity, specifically in relationship to the *Confessions* of the late fourth/early fifth century bishop Augustine of Hippo. This section is not an origin story, has no such interest, but rather an exploration of the fraughtness of interiority.

### Prudentius

The poems attributed to Prudentius (fourth century) are stormy and dramatic, full of stark oppositions and inner conflict, but also periodically full of longing that appears especially in relationship to the natural world. See, for instance, his *Battle of the Soul*, *Hymns for the Martyrs*, and *Hymns for the Hours and Seasons*. Prudentius's moral encoding of light and dark (not uncommon, but especially emphatic) is destructive, and is reflected across Christian literature—including the racialized allegorizing of blackness in Origen of Alexandria's work.

NOTES FOR PART III (*SAINTS' LIVES*)

## Hagiography

The *Life of Constantine* (Eusebius of Caesarea) and the *Life of Antony* (Athanasius of Alexandria) are both variously described as the "beginnings" of hagiography (stories of the lives and deeds of the saints). Biography, especially in antiquity, was always already a little hagiographical, though, full of praise and virtue and accomplishment.

## Slow Death

Berlant's conceptualization of "slow death," now widely circulated and variously critiqued and rethought, comes in the context of their book *Cruel Optimism*, which characterizes a particular affective mood (cruel optimism = desiring something that is an obstacle to your own flourishing) and set of embodied non- or quasi-agential responses to the thinning possibility for upward mobility and the American dream. I draw no direct comparisons between Berlant's post–Reagan era United States and the long era of late antiquity, for either their precise economic and social circumstances or for a single, characterizable, overall mood. Rather, I see "slow death" as a helpful way of naming conditions of attrition. I find in Berlant's discussion of population-wide subjective responses to these conditions of attrition a way to rethink and deromanticize the kinds of changes that we imagine ascetics undergo in the fourth and fifth centuries. Suggesting people experience forms of grief that have textures and expressions specific to their conditions is, to me, quite different from designating a period an "age of anxiety" for instance.[5]

## Simeon

The story of Simeon, also called Simeon Stylites, is the story of a Syrian ascetic who lived for thirty-seven years on a pillar—he built the pillar to escape the crowds who came to see him, to touch him, as a kind of "ascetic celebrity" and tourist destination, as saints often became.[6]

## Antony

Antony of Egypt is the mythologized founder of Egyptian monasticism, which takes off in the late third and early fourth centuries. Athanasius, the bishop of Alexandria, imagines Antony's early life, and describes decades of struggles between Antony and demons in the desert. But Antony begins simply as an obedient child who cares little for material things. It is only when his parents die that he decides to go it alone, selling the family's property, and putting his sister in a convent. The demons tempt him by reminding him of what he left. Athanasius, in other words, tells a story of grief.

### Melania

Melania's story, as told by Gerontius, is of a woman of extreme wealth from a senatorial family. She wanted to live the chaste Christian life, but is forced to marry at fourteen. She was able to convince her husband Pinian to join her in the ascetic life, but only after she agreed to have two children who then grow to care for their property. Both of the children died young. It is only with the death of their children and Melania's father that she and Pinian are able to live as they wish, freed from their family obligations and wealth. Even then, Melania and Pinian still are so overwhelmed by wealth that they spend much of their entire lives trying to give their money and property away. Gerontius's hagiographical tale works equally to launder the reputations of the wealthy through explication of their virtues and their burdens, and also to detail just how steep the obligations to family and property could be in this time.

### Macrina

Macrina's life and great virtues are described by her brother, Gregory of Nyssa, who seems always to be in her shadow even while he is contriving the story. What Gregory admires is that Macrina is steadfast to an uncanny degree. In *On the Soul and Resurrection*, Gregory imagines asking Macrina how to sustain loss, and he begins from the terrible loss of their brother, Basil. In his *Life of Macrina*, Gregory tells another striking story: after Macrina's death, the woman attending Macrina's body shows Gregory a small mark, one made as if by a small needle, on Macrina's breast. The scar, the woman says, marks the place where a tumor once was. It was too dangerous to cut it out, but it was growing close to the heart, and so Macrina cured herself by applying a salve of her own tears, her mother making the sign of the cross over her breast.

### Perpetua

The story of Perpetua's martyrdom comes written as if it is a diary, and her death is portrayed as especially brutal because she is a new, nursing mother. She is put to death alongside the woman she enslaves, Felicity, also a new mother. Perpetua is devised as having steely devotion not just to her faith but to *modesty*, even in the most extreme moments, fixing her hair and clothes before the crowds who are about to watch her die.

### Mary of Egypt

As told by Sophronius of Jerusalem (sixth century), Mary's is the story of a girl who runs away young and spends almost two decades having sex for pleasure, much to the chagrin of both her parents and the author of this tale. By the time she is discovered by a monk, she is naked, badly burned by the sun, and has been living, apparently redeemed, in this brutal life alone in the desert on scant food for forty-seven years.

NOTES FOR PART IV (*THE PASSING WORLD*)

### The Last Oracle at Delphi

Oracles from the god Apollo had been delivered in Delphi, Greece, for over a thousand years before this. The supposed last oracle at Delphi (fourth century CE) is almost certainly not truly the last oracle of Delphi—the sources for the oracle are many centuries later. Indeed its literary poignancy is intensified as a wistful or sentimentalized projection back from another time: a powerful voice's imagined "confession of its own powerlessness."[7]

### Dedications to the Old Gods

Any quick "decline of paganism," like the notion of an empire-wide Christianization program issuing from Constantine (who himself titrated carefully between traditional and Christian deities, at least in iconography), is overstated, if not wrong.[8] Likewise, epigraphic and sculptural remnants of previous eras, when the traditional gods held sway, lived on in the physical landscape of late antiquity even after the power of the traditional gods shrank back.[9] What did people think and feel about these remnants as time passed? These invented dedications play with those paradoxes, not only the paradoxes of idealizing attachments to power and the past, but of documentation and time: the recalcitrance of the past and the slipperiness of time.

### The Desert and Pilgrimage

The desert was vividly imagined, a place of great colonial projection, especially in the literature of late ancient Christianity. It was imagined to be full of demons, strange and even otherworldly creatures, and vast expanses of nothing. Ascetics and their biographers used the desert as a stage for stories of deprivation and cosmic and spiritual contest. But the desert also drew other visitors, sometimes people coming to encounter saints or visit monasteries, sometimes to see or touch some element of biblical stories of the desert. Indeed, biblically associated sites all over, re-valenced with Christian significance as Christianity came to dominate, also drew tourists (pilgrims) who perhaps did or did not find what they were looking for there. In all cases, though, Christians were remapping the region, and placing non-Christians (inhabitants of the Sinai desert, Jews in Jerusalem) into this strained and moralizing narrative frame.

### Augustine's City of God

Augustine's *City of God Against the Pagans* tells the story of two cities, an earthly city and the city of God. Humanity lives bound up in the ambiguity of these two cities, according to Augustine, but in the future, humanity will be judged, and the baptized will live with God forever in the city of God. The *City of God* is, among other things, a potent temporal container for the chaos of a historical moment: it is written just after the sack of Rome by the Visigoths (476 CE), and while Augustine defends Christian rule, defends Christianity against the claim that it is responsible for Rome's fall, he redirects the reader's gaze upward, to a city otherwise, a city not yet, suggesting his own disappointments with the unmet hopes of Christian rule.

### EPILOGUE

### Metamorphoses

Also called "The Golden Ass," a story told by the second century writer Apuleius, about uncanny, unwieldy changes far beyond one's imagination.

# Notes

### INTRODUCTION

1. I had COVID for nine weeks. Soon after, I developed a chronic migraine condition that soaked up many of my days over the course of the writing of this book. The book's form is not incidental to those conditions, either—a kind of "disability as method." Compatibly (in a general sense), see Mills and Sanchez, *Crip Authorship*; and specifically, for a critique of the kinds of cognition privileged by academia, see. Chen, "Brain Fog." So too Jonathan Sterne's *Diminished Faculties*, especially his description of exhaustion, has lived closely with me.
2. Brown, *The Making of Late Antiquity*.
3. The most frequent parallel between the contemporary United States and the Roman empire these days is made via the story of Rome's "fall," a moralizing discourse that not only presumes a clear narrative arc for both the contemporary United States and the Roman empire, but often laments the loss of imperial robustness. As will become apparent, I am trying to resist (and describe) the desire to diagnose grand arcs and delineate periods.
4. Again, on the possibilities of blurry thinking, see Chen, "Brain Fog."
5. Schott, *Christianity, Empire, and the Making of Religion*, epilogue.
6. See especially the posthumously published *Confessions of the Flesh: The History of Sexuality, Volume IV*. But for a schematic and thorough treatment of Foucault's interest in Christian texts and practice, see Clements, "Foucault's Christianities." Foucault influenced Peter Brown's work on late antiquity, as Brown has described in various times and places. See, for instance, Brown, *The Body and Society*, introduction.

7. Cox Miller, *The Poetry of Thought in Late Antiquity*. See also Roberts, *The Jeweled Style*. Both Roberts and Cox Miller have suggested an "aesthetics of discontinuity" in late ancient writing.

8. This project owes something in particular to Virginia Burrus's *Ancient Christian Ecopoetics*, which mixes a handful of her own poems into a collection of thematically linked, lyrical, and sometimes fragmentary essays. Burrus, too, encourages nonlinearity, and draws together the long past, the present, and her own experiences (6–7). Although not in late antiquity studies, and not interested in making historical claims, Anne Carson's genre-busting work is an obvious precedent here.

9. Kotrosits, *Theory, History, and the Study of Religion*. Such work is no less important for the way it erodes the history/reception divide. For my own deconstruction of this divide, see Kotrosits, "Response."

10. So many poetic renditions of ancient themes, myths, or figures, whether in early Christian studies or classics, are undertaken in aggrandizing and romanticizing registers, which serve to reaffirm their status as universal in relationship to something like "the human," or at least naturalize their canonical place. I am aware of this dynamic. I am frustrated by it. I hope to cut through some of it.

11. The characteristic style and obtuseness of academic prose does, after all, have a history, as Edith Hall has shown in "Aristotle's Lost Works."

12. See, for instance, the introduction of the Latin—*inter alia*—in a reviewer's remark on what I'd forgotten in a piece under review: the elegance of the letters, the soft strangeness of the sounds against the specter of my shoddy bibliography. The missing names spill from her mouth like integers. A recitation, a repetition, a bar, among other things.

13. I suppose I was like Carolyn Dinshaw's amateur, or living out Jack Halberstam's "queer art of failure," but it was less exciting than all of that, and much more about class. I got my first job after my PhD as visiting faculty at Amherst College, famous for its poets (Emily Dickinson, for one) if not also its crackling fireplaces, and a school I could not have gotten into let alone afforded as an undergraduate. I arrived on campus to teach, only to realize just how far out of the echelons of literary culture I had truly been.

14. This distinction between observer and participant in the study of religion is part of the genealogy, fantasy, and ongoing presumption of secularism, as so many have pointed out. However, I do not mean to align science or empiricism with modernity over and against art here, since the scientist and the artist are really twin figures of modernity, both of whom loom large in the religious studies imagination.

15. Doty, *Art of Description*, 22–23. See also Audre Lorde's "Poetry Is Not a Luxury." For Lorde, poetry is "the revelation or distillation of experience," and not "sterile word play," 37.

16. I am not a singer, but when I started approaching poetry more fully again, I had dreams about singing. In one, I found myself in a concert hall, a half a step from the stage, dressed for the occasion. The songs I was supposed to sing I hadn't heard in ages. To my surprise they were all in my range, and I only remembered the words once I was singing.

17. Indeed, that patron saint of the study of religion, Émile Durkheim, associated art of all kinds with the forms of religiosity for which he was generating scientific explanations. "It is a well-known fact," he declares, "that games and the major art forms have emerged from religion, and that they long preserved a religious character." *Elementary Forms of Religious Life*, 283.

18. Kotrosits and Given, "*Ars Botanica.*"

19. Most recently: Lincoln, *Apples and Oranges*; Freiberger, *Considering Comparison*; and Hughes, *Comparison*.

20. Winnicott, *Playing and Reality*, 87–88.

21. Christian, "The Race for Theory," 78.

22. Nash, *How We Write Now*.

23. Bruce, *How to Go Mad*, 4.

24. Bruce, *How to Go Mad*, 5–9.

25. Bruce, *How to Go Mad*, 9.

26. Bruce, *How to Go Mad*, 1–2.

27. Bruce, *How to Go Mad*, 5.

28. I have written on this before; see "Darkening the Discipline," chap. 7.

29. I think of Catherine Michael Chin's review of a book in the esteemed *Bryn Mawr Classical Review*, in which Chin met the book's interest in tiny and fragmentary objects in antiquity with his own tiny and fragmentary lyrical reflections on objects. The review received nothing less than a wave of outrage on social media, some of which came out of structural concerns for what reviews mean for authors' professional advancement. But some came in the form of an outrage that was expressed as a critique of a "lazy" or inscrutable review, and carried other heavy valences, given Chin is Asian and trans. Chin's double interest in late antiquity and puppetry/object theater has helped embolden me to write this book, even as I'm painfully aware how our colleagues' responses to Chin's various kinds of mixing of late antiquity with creative play have ranged from fervent admiration to puzzled shrugs to sour derision. See Chin, "The Tiny."

30. I don't disown them, in part, because there are many dimensions of academic prose that I take pleasure in, both as a reader and as a writer. Besides, not all academic prose invests in rationalist conventions to the same extent. I fell in love with a body of literature that we call *theory*, beginning, counterintuitively, with the prose of Judith Butler, less because I understood the arguments (I didn't yet) than because its density of meaning and cadence reminded me of poetry. Many of the academic books that have stayed with me the longest have done so because of these qualities.

31. Schaefer, *Wild Experiment*.

32. Schaefer, *Wild Experiment*, especially 226–27.

33. Kate Stanley describes postsecular style as an emergent response in some scholarship in religious studies to critiques of secularism in the United States as colonial and regulatory force, one that takes a critical position of situatedness and "feeling with." Stanley, "Postsecular Style." Though admittedly the present book's blurs and intimacy with its subjects are much more extreme than in the works Stanley is reviewing. On postsecularism, see Coviello and Hickman, "Introduction."

34. Loveless, *How to Make Art*, 16. From the conclusion: "If the project isn't (only) to ensure our own survival at the level of the individual or the species, if we give up on the pathological narcissism of me-at-all-costs, then how might we, workers in the university, orient ourselves in our current projects of everyday academic life under the sign of the Anthropocene...?" (99–100).

35. Loveless, *How to Make Art*, 37. While I follow Loveless on several fronts, I do sometimes find her romantic in her discussion of multidisciplinarity and its possibilities (or, as she coins the term, "polydisciplinamory").

36. Loveless, *How to Make Art*, 17.

37. Loveless, *How to Make Art*, 19. The quote is from Haraway, *The Companion Species Manifesto*.

38. Consequently, we can easily try out other genres, with other effects, and be no less "true."

39. Thanks to Andrew Jacobs for this articulation of the problem. While narrative history is a recognized and legitimate academic writing form, it is generally still quite traditional in execution: fact-based, restrained, literal, and with little literary flourish.

40. Brekelmans, "The Fall," 152.

41. "Who would one have to be to sit in that normal restfully, to mourn it, or to desire its continuance? We are, in fact, still in that awful normal that is narrativized as minor injustices, or social ills that would get better if some of us waited, if we had the patience to bear it, if we had noticed and were grateful for the miniscule 'progress,' etc.... Well, yes, this is normal, this usual, this ease was predicated on dis-ease. The dis-ease was always presented as something to solve in the future, but for certain exigencies of budget, but for planning, but for the faults of 'those' people, their lack of responsibility, but for all that, there were plans to remedy it, in some future time. We were to hold onto that hope and the suspension of disbelief it required to maintain 'normal.'" Brand, "On Narrative, Reckoning, and the Calculus of Living and Dying."

42. Though perhaps we can see why the attachment: As Keith Moxey has observed of art, some of the captivating effect of verisimilitude is its ability to make a representation seem to stand outside of time, and even transcend the perspectival limits of its maker. Moxey, *Visual Time*, chap. 3.

43. In psychoanalytic theory, reality and fantasy are not opposites. Rather fantasy is the work of reality construction. Melanie Klein, especially, has observed the way fantasies do not dissipate as we age. Klein writes, "Phantasies—becoming more elaborate and referring to a wider range of objects and situations—continue throughout development and accompany all activities; they never stop playing a great part in all mental life." Klein, *Envy and Gratitude*. See Kotrosits, *The Lives of Objects*, introduction. *The Lives of Objects* contains my own contestation of the way the notion of the "real" and realism operates in the study of antiquity, especially via recourse to material culture, as well as my own articulation of the possibilities of "the real" in historical work.

44. We might also think here of the work of Suzanne Césaire on surrealism, colonialism, and the psyche.

45. Eccleston, "Fantasies of Mimnermos," 287.

46. There are so many ways to write. "Argument" is not only an overused but an impoverished one, certainly in academia.

47. Here, too, I would want us to separate *expertise* from *credentialing*. In fact, it seems worth distinguishing expertise from professionalization, so that we might think of expertise not as disciplinary askesis proven through rigid and informational writing styles, but rather expertise as devoted interest, as years of idiosyncratic study, as intimacy with sources and the dead, as community-involved knowledge-sharing.

48. There is no real agreement on what period (or geography) "late antiquity" designates. While Brown's markers for the era have changed over time, his late antiquity is generally housed in the second through eighth centuries. Central to this narrative of transformation is the notion that with Christian culture come *new* developments that bloom in the thousand or so years that follow. Polymnia Athanassiadi's work, on the other hand, understands the developments of this period as fully connected to the globalized Hellenistic culture following the conquests of Alexander. She thus challenges the segmentation and newness implied by this consensus picture of late antiquity. Athanassiadi, *Mutations of Hellenism*. For larger discussion of periodization and change regarding late antiquity, see Testa, *Late Antiquity in Contemporary Debate*.

49. See Ramsay MacMullen's highly regarded *Christianizing the Roman Empire*, or more recently, accounts of the fall of Rome due to climate change and environmental factors, thoughtfully summarized in Kristina Sessa's "The New Environmental."

50. Gibbon, *History of the Decline and Fall of the Roman Empire*.

51. See Hunt, "The Influence of French Colonial Humanism" and "Imperial Collapse."

52. "To put it briefly, late antiquity is modern because it was constituted in relationship with the colonial other, particularly Algeria. It remains modern to the extent that the constituting role of the colony is unacknowledged in the historiography of the field." Hunt, "The Influence of French Colonial Humanism," 274.

53. For more on the exceptionalisms of the field post-"transformation," especially as they appear in the work of Brown and Foucault, and as they are mitigated by some scholars in late antiquity studies, see Kotrosits, *Theory, History, and the Study of Religion*.

54. As Kristina Sessa writes, critiquing the dichotomy of continuity and change, "Indeed one could argue that everything in history is always changing *and* staying the same...." Sessa, "The New Environmental."

55. There is a long and extensive genealogy for the critique of colonialist, imperialist, and capitalist time. A few examples that have influenced my own thinking and have been diffused into this book, beyond Carolyn Dinshaw's work (on which, see below): Chakrabarty, *Provincializing Europe*; Freeman, *Time Binds*; Roitman, *Anti-Crisis*; Rifkin, *Beyond Settler Time*; Puar, *The Right to Maim*; and Azoulay, *Potential History*.

56. Dinshaw, *How Soon Is Now?*, 22.

57. Dinshaw, *How Soon Is Now?*, 23.

58. Likewise, I have taken cues from Dinshaw's theorizing of queer touch across time in *Getting Medieval*.

59. See especially Gribetz, *Time and Difference*. For another history of imperial time and forms of temporal resistance to it, one from an earlier period, see Kosmin, *Time and Its Adversaries*.

60. Jacobs, *The Remains of the Jews*.

61. Gumbs, *M Archive*, xi.

62. Gumbs, *M Archive*, xi.

63. Gumbs, *M Archive*, xi.

64. I borrow the notion of ancient writers' strategies as improvisations from Jacobs, *Epiphanius of Cyprus*.

65. While *M Archive* is obviously a very different kind of reckoning with time, change, and colonialism, Gumbs has helped me feel out and conceptualize this book.

66. Maldonado Rivera, "Method, Ethics, and Historiography."

67. "Chronology emphasizes a succession, the chaining of things one after another. It fosters a language of accumulation and replacement," writes Stefan Tanaka in *History without Chronology*. He writes, "My hope is that in this renewed interrogation of time, scholars, especially historians, first recognize the historicity of chronology as a construct that claims externality and has gained material expression through the clocks, calendars, conceptual forms, and social structures built on them. . . .," 6. Tanaka argues for, among other things, preserving the heterogeneity of time, which includes less mapping (grid and emplotment), and more multiperspectival readings (chap. 3).

68. Maldonado Rivera, "Method, Ethics, and Historiography."

69. Other scholars of antiquity have tentatively suggested anachronism or anachronology as method. On anachronology, see Greenwood, "Thucydideses." Greenwood, interestingly, draws from the work of Anne Carson (*Men in the Off Hours*) in the conclusion of this essay that illustrates authorship's vulnerabilities in time. In James Uden's *Spectres of Antiquity*, he offers the gothic metaphor of "haunting" for the ongoing presence of antiquity, and because this haunting involves aberrations and interruptions of time, "anachrony" is a central dimension (232). On anachronism, see Chalmers, "'Anti-Semitism' before 'Semites'"; and Marchal, *Appalling Bodies*, both of whom still abide by a strong distinction between past and present. A more programmatic treatment is offered by Brooke Holmes in "At the End of the Line." As Holmes writes, "I argue that the challenge posed by anachronism to these value systems lies not only in positing alternative figurations of time but also in drawing attention to the work of valuation itself that is carried out in the description and use of historical time" (62). Holmes, like Maldonado Rivera, uses the language of diaspora, explicitly but also implicitly ("multiple, mutating stories of transhistorical affinity"), and builds on queer historiography (including Dinshaw), as well.

70. It turns out, in fact, that artistic processes have a distinct capacity to accommodate and appreciate this passing, and where the past-as-passing and art meet is in the infrathin. See for instance the descriptions of this concept, coined by Marcel Duchamp, in the work of Manning, *For a Pragmatics of the Useless*, 15–23; and Perloff, *Infrathin*.

71. See Wiegman, "Introduction"; and Nash, *How We Write Now*.

72. I say "ancient historians, in particular" because we are (dare I say) the field least inclined to do so.

73. For an intellectual history of postcolonial critique, which is still marginal, in the study of religion in late antiquity, see Kotrosits, *Theory, History, and the Study of Religion*.

74. These themes (fathers, interiority, saints, the deterioration of traditional cults) are routine ways the field has carved up phenomena of Christian late antiquity. In organizing the book along these lines, my hope is to play with these categories a bit, to rethink them, which is also to explore their power as frames. (As is probably already very clear, I've always been more drawn to playing with frames of legibility than the invention of new taxonomies.)

75. One of the press's reviewers pointed out the deep contrasts between this book, with its interest in condensation and piecemeal accretion, and such tomes, noting too that the pocket-size of Brown's *Making of Late Antiquity* is an exception in Brown's work.

76. The transformation of late ancient Christian ascetic practice has been the predominant assumption of scholarship for decades, most famously Clark, *Reading Renunciation*; and Burrus, *Sex Lives of Saints*. See full bibliography and discussion in Clements, *Sites of the Ascetic Self*, 15.

77. Berlant, *Cruel Optimism*. Across the present book, Berlant figures large, not just for "slow death" but for their larger critique of sovereign agency as fantasy that prevents us from finer description of social and subjective life. For more on Berlant and slow death, see the appendix section on *Saints' Lives*. Elizabeth Povinelli's foundational and field-shaping work on exhaustion is part of the subtext of this book, as well. Povinelli, *Economies of Abandonment*.

PROLOGUE

1. Heyes, *Anaesthetics of Existence*.
2. Heyes, *Anaesthetics of Existence*, 3.
3. Heyes, *Anaesthetics of Existence*, 97.
4. Heyes, *Anaesthetics of Existence*, 97.
5. See Berlant, *Cruel Optimism*.
6. Heyes, *Anaesthetics of Existence*, 98.
7. Heyes, *Anaesthetics of Existence*, 99.
8. Heyes, *Anaesthetics of Existence*, 117.
9. Heyes, *Anaesthetics of Existence*, 117.
10. Grysa, "The Legend."

PART I. FATHERS

1. Jacobs, *Remains of the Jews*, 23.
2. Sarantis, "Arnold Hughes Martin Jones," in Gwynn, *A. H. M. Jones and the Later Roman Empire*, 8. Emphasis mine.

3. Translation from Chadwick and Oulton, *Alexandrian Christianity*, 446–47.

4. Drake, "Origen's Veils."

5. Harrill, "'Exegetical Torture.'" Indeed, so much ancient paper was stretched and rendered animal skin. See, for instance, Holsinger, *On Parchment*.

6. Harrill, "'Exegetical Torture,'" 48.

7. "Origen" means "born of Horus," Horus being an Egyptian deity. Eusebius describes Origen, defensively, as the son of a Christian martyr. Eusebius, *Church History*, Book 6. Some of the material for this essay overlaps with Kotrosits, "Christians and the Making of Christianity in North Africa and Egypt."

8. On alignment with Greek culture and having Alexandrian associations as lending more positive or at least exceptionalist aura than "Egyptian," which regularly read as "uncivilized" or "lawless," see Rowlandson, "Dissing the Egyptians."

9. See Allen, *The Despoliation of Egypt*, especially 225–29. Throughout *On First Principles*, too, Origen suggests some Egyptians could become Israelites and thus enter a higher echelon. On Origen and the superiority and inferiority of various peoples, see den Dulk, "Origen of Alexandria."

10. On Jewishness in relationship to Origen's writing, see Jacobs, *Remains of the Jews*, 60–67.

11. "Some creatures, however, are called 'earthly,' and among these, too, that is, among men, there are no small differences, for some are barbarians, others Greeks, and of the barbarians, some are wilder and fiercer, whereas others more gentle...." *On First Principles* 2.9.3, translation by G. W. Butterworth.

12. Harland, "Climbing the Ethnic Ladder."

13. Ando and Lavan, "Introduction," 3.

14. As Robert Browning notes, "Professor Jones's *Later Roman Empire* is staggering in its size, its erudition, its systematic and exhaustive treatment of its subject matter, and—may one add—its price." Browning, "Declining Rome Surveyed."

15. Jones, *The Later Roman Empire*, vols. 1 and 2. For a full summary of Jones's passages on Roman bureaucracy, see Heather, "Running the Empire," 97–119.

16. See Heather, "Running the Empire," 99, and Sarantis, "Arnold Hugh Martin Jones," in Gwynn, *A. H. M. Jones*, 21.

17. Kelly, "Later Roman Bureaucracy," 173.

18. Kelly, "Later Roman Bureaucracy," 174.

19. She continues, "Clerks recorded the different categories of suspicion in the rubric marked 'recommendation' on official forms. Sometimes these categories were explicitly stamped in the box for 'evidence of good character' on the forms that people used to apply for posts as civil servants or to request special status as British nationals or British-protected persons. They were noted in the endorsement letters for people applying for passports, travel permits from state to state, and on applications for permits to travel to sensitive areas." Berda, *Colonial Bureaucracy and Contemporary Citizenship*, 14.

20. For more on this, see Puar, *The Right to Maim*, Introduction.

21. See Walia, *Border and Rule*.

22. The Theodosian code contained legal statements about heresies. On the rela-

tionship between the *Panarion* and the Theodosian code, see Flower, "'The Insanity of Heretics Must Be Restrained.'"

23. On Epiphanius as ethnographic writer, see Berzon, *Classifying Christians*, and Kotrosits, "From Herodotus to Heresy."

24. See, for instance, Plutarch, *On Superstition*.

25. See Jacobs, *Epiphanius of Cyprus*, 7.

### INTERLUDE

1. A riff on the text by the same name, found in the collection of late ancient Coptic manuscripts, is now referred to as the Nag Hammadi library.

### PART II. NOTES FROM THE INTERIOR

1. Brown, *Making of Late Antiquity*, 95.
2. Victoria Rimell, *The Closure of Space*, 18.
3. Annamaré Kotzé, "Augustine on Himself," 22–29.
4. Translation adapted from R. S. Pine-Coffin, *Saint Augustine*.
5. Confessions 10.5, quoting 1 Cor. 13:12. Adapted from Pine-Coffin, *Saint Augustine*.
6. Augustine, *Exposition of Psalm* 103, Sermon 1.4. My translation. On the paradoxes of seeing in Augustine, see Cain, *Mirrors of the Divine*, chap. 6. On biblical texts as mirror in Augustine's writings on the psalms, see Hofer, "Looking in the Mirror of Augustine's Rule"; and Fiedrowicz, "Introduction." *Augustine's Expositions of the Psalms 1–32*, vol. 1, especially pages 37–39.
7. On Paul's letters, their opacity, and Paul's earliest readers of that opacity (including Origen and Augustine), see Schellenberg, "On Pauline Indeterminacy."
8. Hofer, "Looking in the Mirror of Augustine's Rule."
9. Sigmund Freud, *The Question of Lay Analysis*, 35. What was frustrating to Freud was, in part, that there was no "neat parallelism between male and female sexual development." See also Freud, "Female Sexuality."
10. Ranjana Khanna, *Dark Continents*.
11. Khanna, *Dark Continents*, 49.
12. Khanna, *Dark Continents*, 46–47.
13. Khanna, *Dark Continents*, 52–56.
14. Khanna, *Dark Continents*, 52.
15. Stanley, *Through the Dark Continent*, 2.
16. Sims, *Story of My Life*, 236.
17. Cooper Owens, *Medical Bondage*, 32.
18. In addition to Cooper Owens, see Schuller, *The Biopolitics of Feeling*, chap. 3.
19. Cooper Owens, *Medical Bondage*, 23.
20. Cooper Owens, *Medical Bondage*, 23.
21. Sims, *Story of My Life*, 231.
22. Sims, *Story of My Life*, 29.

23. Sims, *Story of My Life*, 30.

24. Sims, *Story of My Life*, 31.

25. Gregory of Nyssa, *On Virginity*, 11. "Perhaps, then, the treatise has gently led us through examples to the thought of transforming ourselves to something better than we are, and has showed us also that the only way for the soul to be attached to the incorruptible God is for it to make itself as pure as it can. In this way, reflecting as the mirror does, when it submits itself to the purity of God, it will be formed according to its participation in and reflection of prototypal beauty," 41.

26. Ambrose, *On Virginity*, 1.9.45–46. Song of Songs 4.12, quoted here from the New King James Version. On the garden as metaphor and virginity, see Kristi Upson-Saia, "Gregory of Nyssa on Virginity, Gardens."

27. See Hesiod, *Works and Days*, 60–100.

28. Although the imagination of what constituted virginity was always various, and even physical virginity was not universally defined. See Kelto Lillis, *Virgin Territory*.

29. Lillis, *Virgin Territory*, chap. 2. See for instance Origen, *Homilies on Luke*, 14: 7–8.

30. Ambrose, *On Virginity*, 2.2.6.

31. Ambrose, *On Virginity*, 3.3.11.

32. Ambrose, *On Virginity*, 1.8.40–41.

33. Elizabeth Alexander, The Black Interior, 4.

34. Alexander, *Black Interior*, 5.

35. Quashie, *Sovereignty of Quiet*, 22.

36. Quashie, *Sovereignty of Quiet*, 26

### INTERLUDE

1. With the language from Lactantius/Pseudo-Lactantius's poem *The Phoenix*, with debt to William Fletcher's translation in *Ante-Nicene Fathers*, vol. 7, *Fragments of Lactantius* (1885).

### PART III. SAINTS' LIVES

1. Half of the lines adapted from Eusebius's *Life of Constantine*, Chapter LXXII, the Bagster translation, revised by Ernest Cushing Richardson, available at https://sourcebooks.fordham.edu/basis/vita-constantine.asp.

2. Brown, *Cult of the Saints*, 71.

3. Berlant, *Cruel Optimism*, 95.

4. Bryen, "Citizenship and Its Alternatives," 41–68.

5. Doerfler, "Gone but Not Forgotten?"

6. For useful summaries of the political contexts of late antiquity, see Mitchell, *A History of the Later Roman Empire*.

7. On the scale and effect of these plagues, as well as a description of riots in urban centers, see Sessa, *Daily Life in Late Antiquity*.

8. Stathakopoulos, *Famine and Pestilence in the Late Roman and Early Byzantine Empire*, 8.

9. As Peter Brown suggested as part of the context for ascetic practice in *Body and Society*, 6.

10. Berlant, *Cruel Optimism*, 101.

11. That so many Christian ascetic values and practices are fully consonant with Stoic philosophical values and practices is perhaps why so many figures (Gregory of Nyssa, Athanasius, Theodoret, and more) refer to asceticism as a "philosophy." Saints are commonly described as paragons of Stoic self-control. See Valentasis, "Musonius Rufus and Roman Ascetical Theory."

12. *Letter to Olympias* 17.4.1–2. John reels her in, calling her deprivations excessive.

13. *Letter to Olympias* 17.2.2.

14. *Letter to Olympias* 17.2.1.

15. *Letter to Olympias* 17.3.5. On illness as an interpretational conundrum for Christians, see Crislip, *Thorns in the Flesh*, 2012.

16. On saints as worthy of admiration and emulation, see the prologue to Theodoret of Cyrrhus, *A History of the Monks of Syria*; the prologue in Palladius of Aspuna, *Lausiac History*; Athanasius of Alexandria, *On the Incarnation*, 57: 1–15.

17. *Encomium to Egyptian Martyrs*, 5, in Mayer, *Cult of the Saints*, 215.

18. *On Saint Lucian*, 7. Mayer, *Cult of the Saints*, 63–74.

19. Palladius, *Lausiac History*, 3.

20. *Encomium to the Egyptian Martyrs*, 5. Mayer, *The Cult of the Saints*, 216.

21. See Leyerle, *The Narrative Shape of Emotion*, 9.

22. Chrysostom, *Homily on Genesis*, 25.4, in *The Narrative Shape of Emotion*, 5–6. With thanks to Leyerle for her juxtaposition of John's letters to Olympias and his homily on Genesis, although her connections between the two are different.

23. Adapted from Moore and Wilson, *Nicene and Post-Nicene Fathers*; and Roth, *On the Soul and Resurrection*, 2002.

24. See Doerfler, "Holy Households," 71–85.

25. Jerome, *Epistle 108, To Eustochium*.

26. Jerome, *Epistle 39, To Paula*, 6.

27. Jerome, *Epistle 39, To Paula*, 5. Jerome was also doing damage control for his own reputation after Blesilla's death, as Andrew Cain points out, since Blesilla was following the very lifestyle Jerome had commended to her. Cain, *The Letters of Jerome*, 103–4.

28. "Given the linked nature of the Melanias' legacies, let us ... begin by imagining how Melania the Younger, roughly sixteen years old, felt in her grandmother's presence. . . ." Luckritz Marquis, "Namesake and Inheritance," 35.

29. Winerman, "By the Numbers, 1.

30. Puar, *The Right to Maim*, 6–10.

31. Puar, *The Right to Maim*, 6–10.

32. Puar, *The Right to Maim*, 10.

33. I am far from the first to critique institutional "resilience" language as neoliberal, ableist, and capitalist.

34. Berlant, *Cruel Optimism*, 96.

35. Berlant, *Cruel Optimism*, 96.

36. Mahmood, *The Politics of Piety*.

37. Heyes, *Anaesthetics of Existence*.

## PART IV. THE PASSING WORLD

1. Brown, *Making of Late Antiquity*, 2.

2. My translation/adaptation. On the sources, see Gregory, "Julian and the Last Oracle at Delphi," 355–66.

3. Wildly adapted from Duncombe, *Select Works of the Emperor Julian and Some Pieces of the Sophist Libanius*.

4. Julian, *Against the Galileans*, 345.

5. Julian, *Against the Galileans*, 386.

6. Julian, *Hymn to Helios*, 130.

7. Julian, *Hymn to Helios*, 131.

8. Julian, *Hymn to Helios*, 134.

9. Smith, *Julian's Gods*, 1.

10. Smith, *Julian's Gods*, 2.

11. See Julian, *Misopogon*, 351–52. This was the era in which they were *becoming* "the classics." Of special prominence in Julian's education was that stalwart of ancient education, Homer. As Polymnia Athanassiadi writes, "Indeed it was only thanks to this deeply felt sense of the unity and completeness of the Homeric universe that Julian could begin to feel a person; by a clear—if unconscious process ... he began to absorb himself in a world that was in no danger of collapsing overnight, a world in which there was no room for the absurd. Death itself, moral and physical pain and emotional disturbance were here explicable in terms of divine justice. Whenever in later life clouds gathered in the sky above his head, Julian knew where to seek a patch of sunshine." Athanassiadi, *Julian: An Intellectual Biography*, 20.

12. See Elm, *Sons of Hellenism*, 2015.

13. It is debated whether the Column of Constantine implies Helios or Christ, but it seems that perhaps the ambiguity is the point. See discussion in Falcasantos, *Constantinople*, 69, especially note 90.

14. Jacobs, *Remains of the Jews*, 148–50.

15. Gregory is not the only source for this tradition of Julian's interest, however earnest, in rebuilding the temple, including Julian's own letters. Some of the details in Gregory's version are shared by Ephrem of Nisibis 1:16–20; 2:7; 4:18–26. See Levenson, "The Ancient and Medieval Sources." Levenson notes that this story has no Jewish traditions until the sixteenth century.

16. Gregory of Nazianzus, *Second Invective Against Julian*, in King, *Julian the Emperor*, 89.

17. Wilkinson, *Egeria's Travels*, 123.

18. Wilkinson, *Egeria's Travels*, 123.

## APPENDIX

1. See Muehlberger, "On Authors, Fathers, and Holy Men."
2. Johnson, "Lists, Originality, and Christian Time."
3. On a particular convergence of language and women in Jerome's writings, see Cox Miller, "The Blazing Body, 22–45.
4. Jacobs, *Remains of the Jews*, 55–60.
5. Dodds, *Pagan and Christian in an Age of Anxiety*.
6. Jacobs, "'I want to be alone.'"
7. Gregory, "Julian and the Last Oracle at Delphi."
8. See, for instance, Frankfurter, *Christianizing Egypt*.
9. Sitz, *Pagan Inscriptions, Christian Viewers*.

# Bibliography

Alexander, Elizabeth. *The Black Interior: Essays*. Minneapolis: Graywolf Press, 2004.

Alexander, M. Jacqui. *Pedagogies of Crossing: Meditations on Feminism, Sexual Politics, Memory, and the Sacred*. Durham: Duke University Press, 2005.

Allen, Joel Stevens. *The Despoliation of Egypt in Pre-Rabbinic, Rabbinic and Patristic Traditions*. 1st ed. Leiden: Brill, 2008.

Ambrose of Milan. *On Virginity*. Translated by Daniel Callam. Saskatoon: Peregrina, 1987.

Ando, Clifford, and Miles Lavan, eds. *Roman and Local Citizenship in the Long Second Century CE*. New York: Oxford University Press, 2021.

Athanasius of Alexandria. *On the Incarnation*. Translated by John Behr. Yonkers, NY: St. Vladimir's Seminary Press, 2011.

Athanassiadi, Polymnia. *Mutations of Hellenism in Late Antiquity*. Variorum Collected Studies Series, CS 1052. New York: Routledge, 2015.

Athanassiadi, Polymnia. *Julian: An Intellectual Biography*. New York: Routledge, 2014. Reprint.

Augustine of Hippo. *The City of God: A New Translation*. Translated by Marcus Dods. Edinburgh: Clark, 1913.

Augustine of Hippo. *Confessions*. Translated by R. S. Pine-Coffin. New York: Penguin, 1961.

Azoulay, Ariella Aïsha. *Potential History: Unlearning Imperialism*. New York: Verso, 2019.

Berda, Yael. *Colonial Bureaucracy and Contemporary Citizenship: Legacies of Race and*

Emergency in the Former British Empire. Cambridge: Cambridge University Press, 2023.

Berlant, Lauren. *Cruel Optimism*. Durham, NC: Duke University Press, 2011.

Berzon, Todd S. *Classifying Christians: Ethnography, Heresiology, and the Limits of Knowledge in Late Antiquity*. Oakland: University of California Press, 2016.

Brand, Dionne. "On Narrative Reckoning and the Calculus of Living and Dying." *Toronto Star*, July 4, 2020.

Brekelmans, Alana. "The Fall: An Affective Methodology." *Capacious: Journal for Emerging Affect Inquiry* 8 (1) (2023): 143–63.

Brown, Peter. *The Cult of the Saints: Its Rise and Function in Latin Christianity*. Enlarged edition. Chicago: University of Chicago Press, 2015.

Brown, Peter. *The Body and Society: Men, Women, and Sexual Renunciation in Early Christianity*. Twentieth anniversary edition, with a new introduction. New York: Columbia University Press, 2008.

Brown, Peter. *The Making of Late Antiquity*. Cambridge, MA: Harvard University Press, 1978.

Browning, Robert. "Declining Rome Surveyed." *Classical Review* 15 (3) (1965): 335–39.

Bruce, La Marr Jurelle. *How to Go Mad Without Losing Your Mind: Madness and Black Radical Creativity*. Durham, NC: Duke University Press, 2021.

Bryen, Ari. "Citizenship and Its Alternatives: A View from the East." In *Roman and Local Citizenship in the Long Second Century CE*, edited by Myles Lavan and Clifford Ando, 41–68. New York: Oxford University Press, 2022.

Burrus, Virginia. *Ancient Christian Ecopoetics: Cosmologies, Saints, Things*. Philadelphia: University of Pennsylvania Press, 2019.

Burrus, Virginia. *The Sex Lives of Saints: An Erotics of Ancient Hagiography*. Philadelphia: University of Pennsylvania Press, 2010.

Cain, Andrew. *The Letters of Jerome: Asceticism, Biblical Exegesis, and the Construction of Christian Authority in Late Antiquity*. New York: Oxford University Press, 2009.

Cain, Emily R. *Mirrors of the Divine: Late Ancient Christianity and the Vision of God*. New York: Oxford University Press, 2023.

Callahan, Virginia Woods, trans. *Ascetical Works of Saint Gregory of Nyssa*. Washington, DC: Catholic University of America Press, 1967.

Carson, Anne. *Men in the Off Hours*. Toronto, ON: Vintage Canada, 2001.

Césaire, Suzanne. 2012. "1943: Surrealism and Us." In *The Great Camouflage: Writings of Dissent*, edited by Daniel Maximin, translated by Keith L. Walker. Middletown, CT: Wesleyan University Press.

Chadwick, Henry, and John Ernest Leonard Oulton. *Alexandrian Christianity: Selected Translations of Clement and Origen*. The Library of Christian Classics, Volume 2. Philadelphia: Westminster Press, 1954.

Chakrabarty, Dipesh. *Provincializing Europe: Postcolonial Thought and Historical Difference*. Princeton, NJ: Princeton University Press, 2000.

Chalmers, Matthew. "'Anti-Semitism' before 'Semites': The Risks and Rewards of Anachronism." *Public Medievalist*, July 13, 2017.

Chen, Mel Y. "Brain Fog: The Race for Cripistemology." *Journal of Literary and Cultural Disability Studies* 8 (2) (2014): 171–284. https://doi.org/10.3828/jlcds.2014.14.

Chin, Catherine Michael. "Apostles and Aristocrats." In *Melania: Early Christianity Through the Life of One Family*, edited by Catherine Michael Chin and Caroline T. Schroeder Oakland: University of California Press, 2017.

Chin, Catherine Michael. *Grammar and Christianity in the Late Roman World*. Philadelphia: University of Pennsylvania Press, 2007.

Chin, Catherine Michael. Review. *The Tiny and the Fragmented: Miniature, Broken, or Otherwise Incomplete Objects in the Ancient World* by S. Rebecca Martin and Stephanie M. Langin-Hooper. New York: Oxford University Press, 2018. *Bryn Mawr Classical Review* 12(25) (2020).

Chin, Catherine Michael, and Caroline T. Schroeder, eds. *Melania: Early Christianity Through the Life of One Family*. Oakland: University of California Press, 2017.

Christian, Barbara. "The Race for Theory." *Cultural Critique* 6 (1987): 51–78.

Clark, Elizabeth A. *Melania the Younger: From Rome to Jerusalem*. New York: Oxford University Press, 2021.

Clark, Elizabeth A. *Reading Renunciation: Asceticism and Scripture in Early Christianity*. Princeton, NJ: Princeton University Press, 1999.

Clements, Niki Kasumi. "Foucault's Christianities." *Journal of the American Academy of Religion* 89(1) (2021): 1–40.

Clements, Niki Kasumi. *Sites of the Ascetic Self: John Cassian and Christian Ethical Formation*. Notre Dame, IN: University of Notre Dame Press, 2020.

Cobb, L. Stephanie, ed. *The Passion of Perpetua and Felicitas in Late Antiquity*. Translated by Stephanie Cobb and Andrew S. Jacobs. Berkeley: University of California Press, 2021.

Cooper Owens, Deirdre Benia. *Medical Bondage: Race, Gender, and the Origins of American Gynecology*. Athens: University of Georgia Press, 2018.

Coviello, Peter, and Jared Hickman. "Introduction: After the Postsecular." *American Literature* 86 (4) (2014): 645–54.

Crislip, Andrew. *Thorns in the Flesh: Illness and Sanctity in Late Ancient Christianity*. 1st ed. Philadelphia: University of Pennsylvania Press, 2012.

den Dulk, Matthijs. "Origen of Alexandria and the History of Racism as a Theological Problem." *Journal of Theological Studies* 71 (1) (2020): 164–95.

Dinshaw, Carolyn. *Getting Medieval: Sexualities and Communities, Pre- and Postmodern*. Durham, NC: Duke University Press, 1999.

Dinshaw, Carolyn. *How Soon Is Now?: Medieval Texts, Amateur Readers, and the Queerness of Time*. Durham, NC: Duke University Press, 2012.

Dodds, E. R. *Pagan and Christian in an Age of Anxiety: Some Aspects of Religious Experience from Marcus Aurelius to Constantine*. Cambridge: Cambridge University Press, 1965.

Doerfler, Maria E. "Gone but Not Forgotten? Retrieving the Migrant in Late Antiquity." *Journal of the American Academy of Religion* 87 (4) (2019): 1153–77.

Doerfler, Maria E. "Holy Households." In *Melania the Younger: From Rome to Jerusalem* by Elizabeth A Clark. New York: Oxford University Press, 2021.
Doty, Mark. *The Art of Description: World into Word.* Minneapolis: Graywolf, 2010.
Drake, Susanna. "Origen's Veils: The Askēsis of Interpretation." *Church History*, 83 (4) (2014): 815–42.
Duncombe, John. *Selected Works of the Emperor Julian and Some Pieces of the Sophist Libanius*, Volume 2, 1784.
Durkheim, Émile. *The Elementary Forms of Religious Life.* Translated by Carol Cosman. New York: Oxford University Press, 2001.
Eccleston, Sasha-Mae. "Fantasies of Mimnermos in Anne Carson's 'The Brainsex Paintings' (Plainwater)." In *Classical Traditions in Modern Fantasy*, edited by Brett M. Rogers and Benjamin Eldon Stevens, 271–89. New York: Oxford University Press, 2017.
Elm, Susanna. *Sons of Hellenism, Fathers of the Church: Emperor Julian, Gregory of Nazianzus, and the Vision of Rome.* Oakland: University of California Press, 2015.
Eusebius of Caesarea. *The History of the Church.* Translated by Jeremy Schott. Oakland: University of California Press: 2019.
Eusebius of Caesarea. *The Life of the Blessed Emperor Constantine.* Translated by Ernest Cushing Richardson, https://sourcebooks.fordham.edu/basis/vita-constantine.asp. London: S. Bagster and Sons, 1845.
Falcasantos, Rebecca Stephens. *Constantinople: Ritual, Violence, and Memory in the Making of a Christian Imperial Capital.* Oakland: University of California Press, 2020.
Fiedrowicz, Michael. "Introduction." In *Augustine's Expositions of the Psalms 1–32*, vol. 1. El Segundo, CA: New City Press, 1990.
Flower, Richard. "'The Insanity of Heretics Must Be Restrained': Heresiology in the Theodosian Code." In *Theodosius II: Rethinking the Roman Empire in Late Antiquity*, edited by Christopher Kelly, 172–94. Cambridge: Cambridge University Press, 2013.
Foucault, Michel. *Confessions of the Flesh: The History of Sexuality*, Volume 4. Edited by Frederic Gros. Translated by Robert Hurley. New York: Pantheon Books, 2021.
Frankfurter, David. *Christianizing Egypt: Syncretism and Local Worlds in Late Antiquity.* Princeton, NJ: Princeton University Press, 2017.
Freeman, Elizabeth. *Time Binds: Queen Temporalities, Queer Histories.* Durham, NC: Duke University Press, 2010.
Freiberger, Oliver. *Considering Comparison: A Method for Religious Studies.* New York: Oxford University Press, 2019.
Freud, Sigmund. *The Question of Lay Analysis: An Introduction to Psycho-Analysis.* Translated by Nancy Proctor-Gregg. London: Imago, 1947.
Freud, Sigmund. "Female Sexuality." In *The Standard Edition of the Complete Psychological Works of Sigmund Freud: Volume XXI (1927–1931): The Future of an Illusion, Civilization and Its Discontents and Other Works*, 221–44. Edited by James Strachey, Anna Freud, Alix Strachey, and Alan Tyson. London: Hogarth Press: The Institute of Psycho-Analysis, 1931.

Gibbon, Edward. *The History of the Decline and Fall of the Roman Empire*. London: W. Strahan and T. Cadell, 1782.

Goldhill, Simon. *The Christian Invention of Time: Temporality and the Literature of Late Antiquity*. Cambridge: Cambridge University Press, 2022.

Greenwood, Emily. "Thucydideses: Authorship, Anachrony, and Anachronism in Greek Historiography." *Classical Receptions Journal* 12 (1) (2020): 32–45.

Gregory of Nyssa. *On the Soul and Resurrection*. Translated by Catharine P. Roth. Crestwood, NY: St. Vladimir's Seminary Press, 2002.

Gregory, Timothy E. "Julian and the Last Oracle at Delphi." *Greek, Roman, and Byzantine Studies* 24 (4) (1983): 355–66.

Grysa, Bartlomiej. "The Legend of the Seven Sleepers of Ephesus in Syriac and Arab Sources—a Comparative Study." *Orientalia Christiana Cracoviensia*, 2 (2010): 45–59.

Gumbs, Alexis Pauline. *M Archive: After the End of the World*. Durham, NC: Duke University Press, 2018.

Gwynne, David, ed. *A. H. M. Jones and the Later Roman Empire*. Leiden: Brill, 2008.

Halberstam, Jack. *The Queer Art of Failure*. Durham, NC: Duke University Press, 2011.

Hall, Edith. "Aristotle's Lost Works for the Public and the Politics of Academic Form." In *The Politics of Form in Greek Literature*, edited by Phiroze Vasunia, 161–78. London: Bloomsbury Academic, 2022.

Haraway, Donna J. *The Companion Species Manifesto: Dogs, People, and Significant Otherness*. 6th ed. Chicago: Prickly Paradigm Press, 2015.

Harland, Philip A. "Climbing the Ethnic Ladder: Ethnic Hierarchies and Judean Responses." *Journal of Biblical Literature* 138 (3) (2019): 665–86.

Harrill, J. Albert. "'Exegetical Torture' in Early Christian Biblical Interpretation: The Case of Origen of Alexandria." *Biblical Interpretation* 25 (1) (2017): 39–57.

Harvey, Stefan, and Fred Moten. *The Undercommons: Fugitive Planning and Black Study*. New York: Minor Compositions, 2014.

Heather, Peter. "Running the Empire: Bureaucrats, Curials, and Senators." In *A. H. M. Jones and the Later Roman Empire*, edited by D. M. Gwynn, Vol. 15: 97–119. Leiden, NL: Brill, 2008.

Heyes, Cressida J. *Anaesthetics of Existence: Essays on Experience on the Edge*. Durham, NC: Duke University Press, 2020.

Hofer, Andrew. "Looking in the Mirror of Augustine's Rule." *New Blackfriars* 93 (1045) (2012): 263–75.

Holmes, Brooke. "At the End of the Line: On Kairological History." *Classical Receptions Journal* 12 (1) (2020): 62–90.

Holsinger, Bruce. *On Parchment: Animals, Archives, and the Making of Culture from Herodotus to the Digital Age*. New Haven, CT: Yale University Press, 2023.

Hughes, Aaron W. *Comparison: A Critical Primer*. Bristol, UK: Equinox , 2017.

Hunt, Thomas E. "Imperial Collapse and Christianization in Patristic Scholarship during the Final Decades of Colonial Algeria, 1930–1962." *Journal of Early Christian Studies* 29 (2) (2021): 261–89.

Hunt, Thomas E. "The Influence of French Colonial Humanism on the Study of Late Antiquity: Braudel, Marrou, Brown." *International Journal of Francophone Studies* 21 (3) (2018): 255–78.

Jacobs, Andrew S. *Epiphanius of Cyprus: A Cultural Biography of Late Antiquity*. Berkeley: University of California Press, 2021.

Jacobs, Andrew S. "'I want to be alone': Ascetic Celebrity and the Splendid Isolation of Simeon Stylites." In *The Garb of Being: Embodiment and the Pursuit of Holiness in Late Ancient Christianity*, edited by Georgia Frank, Susan R. Holman, and Andrew S. Jacobs, 145–68. New York: Fordham University Press, 2020.

Jacobs, Andrew S. *Remains of the Jews: The Holy Land and Christian Empire in Late Antiquity*. Stanford, CA: Stanford University Press, 2003.

Johnson, Scott Fitzgerald. "Lists, Originality, and Christian Time: Eusebius's Historiography of Succession." In *Historiography and Identity 1: Ancient and Early Christian Narratives of Community*, edited by Walter Pohl and Vernika Weiser, 191–217. Turnhout: Brepols, 2019.

Jones, A. H. M. (Arnold Hugh Martin). *The Later Roman Empire 284–602: A Social, Economic, and Administrative Survey*, Vols. 1 and 2. Baltimore: Johns Hopkins Press, 1986.

Julian the Emperor. *Select Works of the Emperor Julian, and Some Pieces of the Sophist Libanius*. Translated by John Duncombe. London: J. Nichols for T. Cadell, in the Strand, 1784.

Kattan Gribetz, Sarit. *Time and Difference in Rabbinic Judaism*. Princeton, NJ: Princeton University Press, 2020.

Kaufman, Janet A., Anne F. Herzog, and Jan F. Levi, eds. *"The Speed of Darkness": The Collected Poems of Muriel Rukeyser*. Pittsburgh: University of Pittsburgh Press, 2016.

Kelly, C. M. "Later Roman Bureaucracy: Going Through the Files." In *Literacy and Power in the Ancient World*, edited by Alan K. Bowman and Greg Woolf, 161–76. Cambridge; New York: Cambridge University Press, 1994.

Kelly, Christopher, ed. *Theodosius II: Rethinking the Roman Empire in Late Antiquity*. Cambridge: Cambridge University Press. 2013.

Khanna, Ranjana. *Dark Continents: Psychoanalysis and Colonialism*. Durham, NC: Duke University Press, 2003.

King, C. W. *Julian the Emperor*. London: G. Bell and Sons, 1888.

Klein, Melanie. *Envy and Gratitude*. New York: Basic Books, 1957.

Kosmin, Paul J. *Time and Its Adversaries in the Seleucid Empire*. Cambridge, MA: Harvard University Press, 2018.

Kotrosits, Maia. "Christians and the Making of Christianity in North Africa and Egypt." In *The Cambridge History of the African Diaspora*, Vol. 1. Edited by Solange Ashby, Dan-el Padilla Peralta, and Eve Troutt Powell. Cambridge: Cambridge University Press, forthcoming.

Kotrosits, Maia. "From Herodotus to Heresy: Scythians in Long Historical Perspective." In *Markers of Northernness in Antiquity*, edited by Antti Lampinen. (forthcoming.)

Kotrosits Maia. *Theory, History, and the Study of Religion in Late Antiquity: Speculative Worlds*. 1st ed. Cambridge: Cambridge University Press, 2023.

Kotrosits, Maia. "Response: The Blur of Letters, the Residue of Reception." *Biblical Interpretation* 30 (5) (2022): 642–50.

Kotrosits, Maia. *The Lives of Objects: Material Culture, Experience, and the Real in the History of Early Christianity*. Chicago: University of Chicago Press, 2020.

Kotrosits, Maia, and J. Gregory Given, "*Ars Botanica*: Art, Science, and Comparison in Religious Studies." *Method and Theory in the Study of Religion* (July 2025).

Kotzé, Annemaré. "Augustine on Himself." In *Augustine in Context*, edited by Tarmo Toom, 22–29. Washington, DC: Georgetown University Press, 2017.

Lavan, Myles, and Clifford Ando, eds. *Roman and Local Citizenship in the Long Second Century CE*. New York: Oxford University Press, 2022.

Levenson, David. "The Ancient and Medieval Sources for the Emperor Julian's Attempt to Rebuild the Jerusalem Temple." *Journal for the Study of Judaism in the Persian, Hellenistic, and Roman Period* 35 (4) (2004): 409–60.

Leyerle, Blake. *The Narrative Shape of Emotion in the Preaching of John Chrysostom*. Oakland: University of California Press, 2020.

Lillis, Julia Kelto. *Virgin Territory: Configuring Female Virginity in Early Christianity*. Oakland: University of California Press, 2023.

Lincoln, Bruce. *Apples and Oranges: Explorations in, on, and with Comparison*. Chicago: University of Chicago Press, 2018.

Lizzi Testa, Rita, ed. *Late Antiquity in Contemporary Debate*. Newcastle upon Tyne, UK: Cambridge Scholars Publishing, 2017.

Lorde, Audre. "Poetry Is Not a Luxury." In *Sister Outsider: Essays and Speeches*, 37. Berkeley, CA: Crossing Press, 1984.

Loveless, Natalie. *How to Make Art at the End of the World: A Manifesto for Research-Creation*. 1st ed. Durham, NC: Duke University Press, 2019.

Luckritz Marquis, Christine. "Namesake and Inheritance." In *Melania: Early Christianity Through the Life of One Family* by Chin and Schroeder. Oakland: University of California Press, 2017.

Lyerle, Blake. *The Narrative Shape of Emotion in the Preaching of John Chrysostom*. Oakland: University of California Press, 2020.

MacMullen, Ramsay. *Christianizing the Roman Empire: (A.D. 100–400)*. New Haven, CT: Yale University Press, 1984.

Mahmood, Saba. *Politics of Piety: The Islamic Revival and the Feminist Subject*. Princeton, NJ: Princeton University Press, 2011.

Maldonado Rivera, David. "Method, Ethics, and Historiography: A Late Ancient Caribbean in the Temporalities of Empire." *Ancient Jew Review*, January 25, 2022.

Manning, Erin. *For a Pragmatics of the Useless*. Durham, NC: Duke University Press, 2020.

Marchal, Joseph A. *Appalling Bodies: Queer Figures Before and After Paul's Letters*. New York: Oxford University Press, 2019.

Mayer, Wendy. *The Cult of the Saints: Select Homilies and Letters of John Chrysostom*.

Translated and introduced by Wendy Mayer with Bronwen Neil. Crestwood, NY: St. Vladimir's Seminary Press, 2006.

McCormick, Michael. "Tracking Mass Death During the Fall of Rome's Empire (I)." *Journal of Roman Archaeology* 29 (2015): 325–57. https://doi.org/10.1017/S1047759415002512.

Miller, Patricia Cox. *The Poetry of Thought in Late Antiquity: Essays in Imagination and Religion*. New York: Routledge, 2001.

Miller, Patricia Cox. "The Blazing Body: Ascetic Desire in Jerome's Letter to Eustochium." *Journal of Early Christian Studies* 1 (1) (1993): 21–45.

Mills, Mara, and Rebecca Sanchez, eds. *Crip Authorship: Disability as Method*. New York: New York University Press, 2023.

Mitchell, Stephen. *A History of the Later Roman Empire, AD 284–641*. Second edition. Malden, MA: Wiley Blackwell, 2015.

Moore, Williams, and Henry Austin Wilson. *Nicene and Post-Nicene Fathers, Second Series*. Volume 5. Edited by Philip Schaffe and Henry Wace. Buffalo, NY: Christian Literature Publishing, 1893.

Moxey, Keith P. F. *Visual Time: The Image in History*. Durham, NC: Duke University Press, 2013.

Muehlberger, Ellen. "On Authors, Fathers, and Holy Men." *Marginalia Review of Books*, September 20, 2015.

Nash, Jennifer C. *How We Write Now: Living with Black Feminist Theory*. Durham, NC: Duke University Press, 2024.

O'Daly, Gerard. *Days Linked by Song: Prudentius' Cathemerinon*. New York: Oxford University Press. 2012.

Origen of Alexandria. *On First Principles*. Translated by G. W. Butterworth. Eugene, OR: Wipf and Stock, 2012.

Palladius of Aspuna. *The Lausiac History*. Translated by John Wortley. Athens, OH: Cistercian Publications, 2015.

Perloff, Marjorie. *Infrathin: An Experiment in Micropoetics*. Chicago: University of Chicago Press, 2021.

Pine-Coffin, R. F. *Saint Augustine: Confessions*. New York: Penguin Books, 1961.

Plutarch. *Moralia, Volume II*. Translated by Frank Cole Babbitt. Loeb Classical Library 222. Cambridge, MA: Harvard University Press, 1928.

Povinelli, Elizabeth. *Economies of Abandonment: Social Belonging and Endurance in Late Liberalism*. Durham, NC: Duke University Press, 2011.

Puar, Jasbir K. *The Right to Maim: Debility, Capacity, Disability*. Durham, NC: Duke University Press, 2017.

Quashie, Kevin Everod. *The Sovereignty of Quiet: Beyond Resistance in Black Culture*. New Brunswick, NJ: Rutgers University Press, 2012.

Rampell, Catherine. "The Trump administration's Kafkaesque new way to thwart visa applications." *Washington Post*, February 18, 2020.

Rifkin, Mark. *Beyond Settler Time: Temporal Sovereignty and Indigenous Self-Determination*. Durham, NC: Duke University Press, 2017.

Rimell, Victoria. *The Closure of Space in Roman Poetics: Empire's Inward Turn*. Cambridge: Cambridge University Press, 2015.

Roberts, Michael. *The Jeweled Style: Poetry and Poetics in Late Antiquity*. Ithaca, NY: Cornell University Press, 1989.

Roitman, Janet L. *Anti-Crisis*. Durham, NC: Duke University Press, 2013.

Roth, Catherine. *On the Soul and Resurrection: Gregory of Nyssa*. Crestwood, NY: St. Vladimir's Seminary Press, 2002.

Rowlandson, Jane. "Dissing the Egyptians: Legal, Ethnic, and Cultural Identities in Roman Egypt." *Bulletin of the Institute of Classical Studies*, Supplement no. 120 (2013): 213–47.

Sarantis, Alexander. "Arnold Hugh Martin Jones." In *A. H. M. Jones and the Later Roman Empire*, edited by D. M. Gwynn, Vol. 15: 1–24. Leiden, NL: Brill, 2008

Schaefer, Donovan O. *Wild Experiment: Feeling Science and Secularism After Darwin*. Durham, NC: Duke University Press, 2022.

Schaff, Philip, and Henry Wace, eds. *A Select Library of Nicene and Post-Nicene Fathers of the Christian Church, Second Series*, Volume 5. Buffalo, NY: Christian Literature Publishing, 1893.

Schellenberg, Ryan S. "On Pauline Indeterminacy." In *Recovering an Undomesticated Apostle: Essays on the Legacy of Paul*, edited by Christopher B. Zeichmann and John A. Egger, 277–304. Kingston, ONT: McGill-Queens's University Press, 2023.

Schott, Jeremy M. *Christianity, Empire, and the Making of Religion in Late Antiquity*. Philadelphia: University of Pennsylvania Press, 2008.

Schott, Jeremy M. *Eusebius of Caesarea; The History of the Church: A New Translation*. Oakland: University of California Press, 2019.

Schuller, Kyla. *The Biopolitics of Feeling: Race, Sex, and Science in the Nineteenth Century*. Durham, NC: Duke University Press, 2017.

Sessa, Kristina. *Daily Life in Late Antiquity*. New York: Cambridge University Press, 2018.

Sessa, Kristina. "The New Environmental Fall of Rome: A Methodological Consideration." *Journal of Late Antiquity* 12 (1) (2019): 211–55.

Sims, J. Marion. *The Story of My Life*. New York: Da Capo Press, 1968.

Sitz, Anna M. *Pagan Inscriptions, Christian Viewers: The Afterlives of Temples and Their Texts in the Late Antique Eastern Mediterranean*. New York: Oxford University Press, 2023.

Smith, Rowland B. E. *Julian's Gods: Religion and Philosophy in the Thought and Action of Julian the Apostate*. New York: Routledge, 1995.

Stanley, Henry Morton. *Through the Dark Continent, or, The Sources of the Nile Around the Great Lakes of Equatorial Africa and Down the Livingstone River to the Atlantic Ocean*. London: Sampson Low, Marston, Searle & Rivington, 1878.

Stanley, Kate. "Postsecular Style." *American Literary History* 33 (1) (2021): 191–205.

Stathakopoulos, Dionysios. *Famine and Pestilence in the Late Roman and Early Byzantine Empire: A Systematic Survey of Subsistence Crises and Epidemics*. New York: Routledge, 2004.

Sterne, Jonathan. *Diminished Faculties: A Political Phenomenology of Impairment.* Durham, NC: Duke University Press, 2022.

Tanaka, Stefan. *History without Chronology.* Ann Arbor, MI: Lever Press, 2019.

Testa, Lizzi, ed. *Late Antiquity in Contemporary Debate.* Cambridge: Cambridge Scholars Publishing, 2017.

Theodoret of Cyrus. *A History of the Monks of Syria.* Translated by Richard Price. Kalamazoo, MI: Cistercian Publications, 1985.

Uden, James. *Spectres of Antiquity: Classical Literature and the Gothic, 1740–1830.* New York: Oxford University Press, 2020.

Upson-Saia, Kristi. "Gregory of Nyssa on Virginity, Gardens, and the Enclosure of the Paradeisos." *Journal of Early Christian Studies* 27 (1) (2019): 99–131.

Valentasis, Richard. "Musonius Rufus and Roman Ascetical Theory." *Greek, Roman and Byzantine Studies* 40 (1999): 207–31.

Vodoklys S.J., Edward. "John Chrysostom, Letters to Olympias 9, 12, and 17." In *The Cambridge Edition of Early Christian Writings,* 86–106. New York: Cambridge University Press, 2017.

Walia, Harsha. *Border and Rule: Global Migration, Capitalism, and the Rise of Racist Nationalism.* Chicago: Haymarket Books, 2021.

Weigman, Robyn. "Introduction: Autotheory Theory." *Arizona Quarterly* 76 (1) (2020): 1–14.

Whelan, Robin. *Melania: Early Christianity through the Life of One Family. Christianity in Late Antiquity,* 2. Review. *Bryn Mawr Classical Review* 5 (37) (2017). https://bmcr.brynmawr.edu/2017/2017.05.37/.

White, Hayden. *Metahistory: The Historical Imagination in Nineteenth-century Europe.* Baltimore, MD: Johns Hopkins University Press, 1973.

Wilkinson, John. *Egeria's Travels.* 3rd ed. Warminster: Aris and Phillips, 1999.

Winerman, Lea. "By the Numbers: An Alarming Rise in Suicide." *American Psychological Association* 50 (1) (2019): 80.

Winnicott, D. W. *Playing and Reality.* New York: Routledge, 1991